SUMNER COUNTY, TENNESSEE

INVENTORIES, SETTLEMENTS, AND GUARDIAN ACCOUNTS

VOLUME A

MARCH 1808 – FEBRUARY 1821

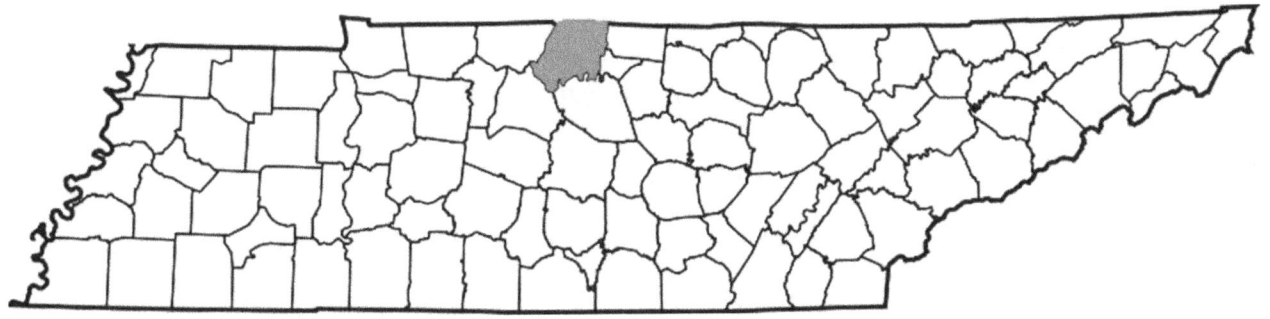

Abstracted by

Mrs. Gale Williams Bamman, Certified Genealogist Emeritus
and
Mrs. Debbie Williams Spero

Copyright ©1984, Mrs. Gale Williams Bamman

Abstracted from a microfilm copy of the original by

Mrs. Gale Williams Bamman, Certified Genealogist Emeritus
and
Mrs. Debbie Williams Spero

All rights reserved

Reprinted
With written permission from Gale W. Bamman

Janaway Publishing Inc.
Santa Maria, California

2023

ISBN: 978-1-59641-482-2

Made in the United State of America

FOREWORD

Although Sumner County, Tennessee was created in 1787 and its wills survive from 1788, the first surviving book of inventories, settlements, and guardian accounts dates only from March 1808.

In an effort to abstract all data that would be of genealogical importance, while at the same time eliminating the many lists of names of buyers at sales, creditors, commissioners, etc., all names were omitted EXCEPT those of the same surname as that of the deceased or minor heir or executor/administrator.

For example, in the abstracting of page one -- the sale of the estate of James WILSON, Sr., dec'd., the names of buyers or creditors other than those with the surname WILSON were omitted. The researcher should keep this in mind, and if the other surnames are desired, he or she should refer to the original record.

One exception to this was the abstracting of all female names, whenever found. Since it was unusual for a female, other than the widow, to be a buyer at an estate sale in those early days, the reference to any females becomes a possible clue and may suggest a kinship with the deceased.

The researcher, with the above in mind, must realize that the appearance of another person with the same surname as the deceased in the probate records does NOT prove relationship or kinship. Only when the records state that there is a division to be made among the heirs, or that persons so named are the heirs of the deceased, will the researcher have evidence of relationship.

It is hoped that few errors will be found in this abstracting. The records have been examined several times in an attempt to make this data as accurate as possible. Should there be any question as to the accuracy of any entry, the researcher is advised to request a copy of that page from the Tennessee State Library and Archives.

Mrs. Gale Williams Bamman

Mrs. Debbie Williams Spero

SUMNER COUNTY, TN INVENTORIES AND SETTLEMENTS
MARCH 1808 - FEBRUARY 1821

Page 1 MARCH TERM 1808

Sale of estate of JAMES WILSON, SR., dec'd. March Term 1808. Buyers:......Hannah Wilson, Samuel Wilson, Zacheus Wilson, Sr., Jonathan Wilson, David Wilson, Zacheus Wilson, Jr. Admr.: Jacob Houd (?).

Page 2

Sale of estate of JOHN WYLES, 20 March 1807. Buyers... William Wyles, Sarah Wyles.

Page 3

Sale of estate of JAMES KELLEY, dec'd. 1 January 1808, by Micajah House, Admr. Buyers....John House.

Page 4

Inventory of sale of estate of ALEXANDER KIRKPATRICK, de'cd. 1 January 1808, by James Kirkpatrick and Hugh Kirkpatrick, Admrs. Buyers: Fanny Kirkpatrick, David Kirkpatrick, Alexander Kirkpatrick, Hugh Kirkpatrick, Joseph Kirkpatrick.

Page 5

Sale of estate of THOMAS PERRY, 5 November 1807. Buyers: George Perry, Catherine Perry, Josiah Perry. George Perry and Catherine Perry, Executors.

Page 7

Sale of estate of WALTER SULLIVAN, 1 January 1806; Buyers: widow Sullivan, John Sullivan. By King Carr and John Sulivent.

Page 8

Inventory of William COCHRAN, dec'd: 1807 Amt. of hire of negroes and rent of plantation; Major Thomas Murry, hire of two negro boys - $105; Joshua Bradly, hire of one negro girl; Henry Gamble, hire of one negro girl; plantation rented to Hum Bate. 1808: Rent of Negro boy Tom to Major Murray; rent of Negro woman to Loftin Cage; rent of negro woman to Patrick Youree; rent of plantation of Loftin Cage. By William Hubert and John Cochran.

Page 8

Supplementary accounting of sale of estate of GEORGE ROBERTS, dec'd. "List of property belonging to estate of Roberts of Sumner Cty, TN that was rec'd in State of Georgia by Rachel Roberts, his admrx." Sold at Greenfield, 16 January 1808. Buyers: Rachel Roberts, Salley Roberts, John Roberts, Henry Roberts.

(Pages 9-12 are not surviving.)

Page 13 JUNE TERM 1808

Sale of estate of JOHN JOSEY, dec'd., 23 April 1808. Buyers: Patsey Josey, Allen Josey, Edward Douglass, David Hall, Adam Hunter, Hugh Shaw, etc. Edward Douglass, admr.

Page 14

Inventory of William BRACKEN, dec'd., 25 March 1808, by James Bracken, admr.: 200 acres, three Negroes, etc.

Page 15-16

Sale of estate of ABRAHAM HASSELL, dec'd., 8 April 1808. Buyers: Christian Hassell, John Hassell, Genet Hassell. Moore Stephenson, admr.

Page 17

Sale of estate of SAMUEL ARMSTRONG, dec'd., 4 April 1808, by Abel Brandon and John Knox, admrs.

Page 18

Statement of settlement of Dr. EPHRAIM WELLS, dec'd., by Capt. Joseph Hodge, admr.

Page 19   SEPTEMBER TERM 1808

Settlement of estate of JOHN WYLES, dec'd. by Samuel Dorris, admr. 24 March 1808. (Debts exceed credits by $21.00.)

Inventory of estate of WILLIAM PHIPPS, JR., 10 September 1808, by Humphrey Mires, admr.

Page 20

Settlement of estate of ORMAN ALLEN, dec'd. by James Cryer and Isaac Walton, execs. 22 September 1808.

Settlement of estate of SAMUEL ARMSTRONG, dec'd. by Abel Brandon, execr. Cash paid out to....Elizabeth Armstrong $120.00; Magdalene Armstrong $106.53. ....Balance due estate $819.89½.

Settlement of estate of NATHANIEL GILMORE, dec'd., by James and Zacheus Wilson, execrs. 17 September 1808.

Page 21

Settlement with guardians for heirs of HENRY LOVING, dec'd. Guardians: William Maxey and James Douglass. 16 November 1797: notes put in their hands for collection $698.53......... Four years' rent of the plantation with interest: $251.25. Payments made at settlement 23 June 1804: $132.82½. "There will be due each legatee $1,440.37 on 27 September, which it has been stated to us that the last legatee will be of age."

Page 22   DECEMBER TERM 1808

Sale of estate of WILLIAM PHIPPS, JR., 6 October 1808. Buyers: Elizabeth Phipps, Mary Willis. Humphrey Mires, admr.

Page 23

Inventory of estate of Willie CARROLL, dec'd., by Elizabeth Carroll and Robert Gardner.

Page 24

Inventory of estate of WILLIAM BROWN, dec'd. 10 December 1808. by Nancy Brown and William Dorris. "Edward Givens bond to make a deed for 120 acres of land."

Page 25

Inventory of estate of JESSE WELLS, dec'd., 19 December 1808. Debit on Ephriam Rease living in Christian Cty, KY, and on a quantity of corn on the plantation of Thomas Keefe. By James McKain, admr.

Sale of estate of JOHN SEAWELL, dec'd 30 November 1808. (Buyers not listed.) (Also),Account of sale in 1801.

Page 26

Sale of estate of JAMES WHITE, JR., dec'd., by Robert Hall, admr. Buyers: William White, Narcissa White, John White, Joseph White.

Page 27

Settlement of estate of MAJOR JAMES WHITE, JR., by Robert Hall, admr., 13 December 1808. "From 2 October 1806 until 12 December 1808: cash paid out....to Robert White-$2.00, John White-$15.08, Eli White-$25.00, Archibald White-$34.98. Balance due estate $638.23."

Page 28

Inventory of JOHN C. HENDERSON, dec'd. (includes) 3 Negroes. by Edness Henderson, admr. 17 December 1808.

Page 29   MARCH TERM 1809

Sale of estate of WILLIAM BROWN, by William Dorris, admr. Buyers: Nancy Brown, Polly Brown.

Page 30-31

Sale of estate of JAMES SIMPSON, dec'd., by Robert Simpson, admr. Buyers: Robert Simpson, Isaac Simpson, Elizabeth Simpson, widow Simpson, Charles Simpson, E. Simpson, Elijah Simpson, John Simpson, Nancy Simpson. 20 July 1806.

Page 32

Inventory of estate of JAMES WILSON, dec'd., by John Parson, admr. (includes) 5 Negroes.

Page 33

Inventory of estate of GEORGE DUTY, 6 March 1809, by George Gillispie and Eliza Duty, admr and admrx. (includes) 5 negroes and 214 acres.

Page 34

Inventory of estate of NICHOLAS BOYCE, dec'd., by Archibald Marlin, admr. Notes on Robert Boyce, Richard Boyce. "a Negro man who ran away on night of 14 January 1808."

Page 35

Sale of estate of WILLIE CARROLL, dec'd. Buyers: James Carroll, widow Carroll.

Supplemental Acctg. of Sales of estate of JOHN JOSEY, dec'd., 27 January 1809. One Negro man. By Edward Douglass, admr.

Page 36

Supplemental inventory of estate of JESSE WELLS, dec'd., 22 March 1809. 1 Negro. By James McKain, admr.

Settlement with Walton and Gardner, guardians of heirs of Bryant Gardner, dec'd. 1807: property- 1 tract of land rented one year $50.00; 5 Negroes hired. (same for 1808)"The expense of Allen Gardner in 1807 and 3 months in 1806: 15 months boarding-$25.00, schooling 12 months $6.66, clothes,etc.- $49.16 total. Expenses 1808-$42.62. William Gardner's expenses - 1807: $35.95. 1808-$40.00. "Keeping Martin Gardner, Sally Gardner and Betsy Gardner the years 1807 and 1808 - $120.00. Schooling Martin Gardner 6 months $3.33." 15 March 1809.

Page 37
Settlement with admr. of estate of James KELLY, dec'd., by Micajah House, admr. "We find in admr.'s hand a bill of the sale of James Kelly, dec'd. est.- $132.46. Balance due heirs - $43.80." 14 March 1809.

Page 38
Settlement with execs of WILLIAM COCHRAN, dec'd., by William Hubbert and John Cochran, execs. Cash paid out to John Cochran, David Cochran....

Page 39
Division of estate of WILLIAM COCHRAN, dec'd., 7 January 1809. December 1808: divided amongst the several legatees as follows: 1. 100 acres, bds James Winchester, including the home plantation, to the widow. 2. Negro man Tom allotted to Ann Cochran. 3. Negro boy, Peter allotted to Sally Cochran. 4. 2 negresses Lindy and Franky to Rachel Cochran. 5. Negro woman, Pat and her mal child David, to Julia Fryet. 6. 103 acres being balance of original tract after laying off Lot #1, and a negro woman, Lyd to Hiram Cochran.

Page 40   JUNE TERM 1809
Division of Negro property of ABRAHAM HASSELL, dec'd. between the legatees, to wit between the wife of William King and Gennett Hassell. 9 January 1809.

Inventory of estate of RUTH OZBROOKS,dec'd., 27 acres on Dry Fork of Drakes Creek. By William Grainger.

Inventory of RICHARD CAVIT, dec'd., by William Kirkpatrick, "one of the securities of John Cavitt for the administration."

Page 41-44
Inventory of the estate of ROBERT PATTON,dec'd., 15 June 1809, by Robert Patton, execr. 1 Negro girl.

Sale of estate of NICHOLAS BOYCE, dec'd. 14 April 1809. Buyers: Nancy Boyce, William Boyce, John Boyce, Richard Boyce, Nicholas Boyce. By Archibald Marlin, admr.

Page 45
Sale of estate of JAMES WILSON, dec'd, 13 April 1809. Buyers: James Wilson, Elenor Wilson, Moses Wilson, Cinthey Wilson. By John Parson.

Page 46
Sale of estate of GEORGE DUTY, 25 May 1809. ..."with the property especially received and given for the support of the widow and orphans for one year." By George Gillespie, admr. and Eliza Duty, admrx. Buyers: Eliza Duty, William Duty, widow Duty, Solomon Duty.

Page 47
Laying off to Eliza DUTY, relict of GEORGE DUTY, dec'd., one year's provision for the support of her family. 19 June 1809.

Page 48
Inventory of estate of Watson Goostree and Elizabeth Goostree, by guardians Jesse Sheen and Stephen Treble. 23 June 1809.

Settlement with Robert Simpson, admr. of estate of JAMES SIMPSON, dec'd., by order of December Term. Several accts against the estate: Charles Simpson, Robert Simpson.

Page 49
Settlement of estate of ABRAHAM HASSELL, dec'd. Notes(on several including) Christian Hassell, Gennett Hassell, John Hassell, Sr., Benjamin Hassell. By Capt. Moore Stephenson and William Montgomery, Esq., admrs.

Page 50
Settlement with executors of HUGH ELLIOTT, dec'd., John Withers and James Trousdale."...allowances to execs. for their services from 26 October 1802 to June 1809.

Page 51   SEPTEMBER TERM 1809
Inventory of estate of JAMES CLARK, dec'd. (includes several) Negroes. by Mary Clark, William Anderson, and Joseph Hodge, excrs.

Page 52
Inventory of estate of ZACHEUS WILSON, dec'd. September 12, 1809. 3 Negroes. by John Wilson and William Wilson, admrs.

Inventory of estate of Daniel Sanders, dec'd.: 123 1/3 acres, 2 negroes. 2 September 1809.

Page 53
Sale of estate of ELIAS MORRISON, dec'd., by James Stewart, exr. Buyers: Jane Morrison.

Page 54
Sale of estate of WILLIAM McCLELLAND, dec'd., by John Sloan and William Simpson, admrs. Buyers: Mary McClelland, Hugh McClelland.

Page 55-56
Sale of estate of WILLAIM BRACKEN, dec'd., by William Bracken for James Bracken, admr. 20 July 1808. 200 acres, 3 negroes.

Page 57
Supplemental Inventory of estate of BALESS HOUSE, dec'd. 9 August 1807. "Money brought from State of North Carolina by Daniel Green-$450.00". By allen Purvis, execr.

                                           DECEMBER TERM 1809
Sale of estate of ROGER DANIEL, dec'd, by David Green. Buyers: Susannah Daniel.

Page 58
Supplemental Inventory of BALESS HOUSE, dec'd., by Allen Purvis. Hire of Negroes- 1808 and 1809.

Page 59
Sale of estate of RUTH OZBROOKS, dec'd., by William Grainger, exr. Buyers: Michael Ozbrooks.

Page 60
Supplemental accounting of sale of estate of GEORGE DUTY, dec'd., by George Gillespie and Eliza Duty, admrs. Buyers: Weddo Duty.

Page 61
Sale of estate of DANIEL SANDERS, dec'd., by James Sanders and Jane Sanders, admrs. 10 October 1809. Buyers: Jane Sanders, Richard Sanders, James Sanders, Robert Sanders, William Sanders, Jr.

Page 62-65
Sale of estate of ZACHEUS WILSON, dec'd., by John Wilson. Buyers: Samuel Wilson, William Wilson, John Wilson, David Wilson, James C. Wilson, Jonathan Wilson, Betsy Wilson, Matilda Wilson, Jane Wilson, Zacheus Wilson.

Page 66
Supplemental Inventory of BALISS HOUSE, dec'd., by Thomas House. "Cash rec'd by Thomas House in North Carolina 20 October 1808."

Inventory of estate of MATHEW BROWN, dec'd., by Jackson N. Brown, excr., 11 December 1809.

Schedule of property of the orphans of Bryant Gardner, dec'd.: Allen Gardner, William Gardner, and Martin Gardner. Land Rents and Tuition Fees.

Page 67   MARCH TERM 1810
Inventory of estate of WILLIAM KENNEDY, dec'd., by A. W. Kennedy and John Perry.

Page 68
Sale of estate of WATSON GOOSTREE AND ELIZABETH GOOSTREE, orphans. Buyers: Watson Goostree. By Jesse Sheen and Stephen Treble.

Page 69-70
Inventory of estate of MOSES CUMMINS, dec'd., 21 December 1809. Land: 166 2/3 acres. Negroes: 3. By William Edwards, Jr. and John Cotton.

Page 71
Settlement with William Douglas, admr. of FANNY HOWEL, dec'd.

Inventory of hire of negroes belonging to estate of JAMES WILSON, dec'd. By John Parson, admr.

Page 72
Inventory of estate of DANIEL STEWART, dec'd., by Andrew Buckham, admr. "One negro in dispute."

Inventory of estate of WILLIAM PHIPPS, dec'd., by James Cryer. Two negroes.

Page 73   JUNE TERM 1810
Inventory of hire of negroes of estate of WILLIAM COCHRAN, dec'd. by John Cochran. For 1809 and 1810: 5 negroes. (The words, "SMITH COUNTY" are written to the left of John Cochran's name.)

Division of certain Negroes between certain legatees of ROBERT HOBDY, dec'd., per order of court March 1810. To: Patience Cartwright, Lethy Byrn, Bethy Hobdy.

Page 72 (misnumbered)
Settlement with guardians of WATSON GOOSTREE AND ELIZABETH GOOSTREE, Jesse Sheen and Stephen Treble.

Page 73 (misnumbered)
Settlement with admr of WILLIAM CATHEY, dec'd, James Cathey. "Paid to Elizabeth Cathey, heir $514.47 (of $559.45) by James Hart and Charles Donoho."

Page 74
Settlement with exrs. of ROBERT HARRIS, dec'd., Greenberry Orr and Blair Harris, exrs. "Cash paid to....Patsey S. Harris, E. H. Harris, Martha Harris, M. G. Harris...total $50.00. 22 December 1809.

Page 75-76
Settlement with exrs. of BALISS HOUSE, dec'd. 22 December 1809. Allen Purvis and Thomas House, excrs. January 9, 1807 to January 1, 1809:........"Certificate of clerk of the court empowering D. Green to collect money in North Carolina - $1.00 (cost); boarding George House 9½ monts, also washing and mending-$39.52; boarding Baliss House 6 January 1808 til February 1809-$40.00; boarding William House 10 March 1807 til 24 January 1808-$40.00; hiring out the Negroes 1808 and 1809; one pair of shoes for James House - $1.75; boarding James House 1 month $3.33. James McKain's amt for boarding, making, washing and mending-12 months $120.68; Joel Brown's(costs)-$51.00.

Page 77
Inventory of sale of of estate of WILLIAM F. McNUTT, dec'd, by exr.(not named). Inventory of goods and chattels and tenements belonging to firm of McNutt and Findlay, Company, of Gallatin, 30 August 1809. Eight Negroes.

Page 78   SEPTEMBER TERM 1810
Inventory of estate of CHARLES ELLIOTT, dec'd. by exr.(not named). 16 September 1810. 9 Negroes. By Eliza and James Elliott, admrs.

Settlement with Humphrey Miers, admr of WILLIAM PHIPPS, JR., 24 August 1810.

Page 79
Inventory of estate of ANN GREER, dec'd., by John and Joseph Motheral. Notes on James Greer, A. Greer.

Page 80
Supplemental Inventory of CHARLES ELLIOTT, dec'd., by Eliza Elliott, and James Elliott, admrs. 1 negro child.

Page 81
Inventory of estate of THOMAS MARTEN, dec'd, by Agnes Marten, exr. 4 Negroes.

Inventory of estate of DRURY WALTON, dec'd., November 17, 1810. by Gracey(?) Walton. 17 slaves.

Page 82 — DECEMBER TERM 1810
Sale of estate of Charles ELLIOTT, dec'd. Buyers: George Elliott, James Elliott.

Page 83
Settlement of estate of William BRACKEN, dec'd, by James Bracken, admr.

MARCH TERM 1811

Inventory of estate of HENRY YOUNG, dec'd., 22 December 1810. 136 acres.

Page 84-85
Inventory and sale of estate of Nathaniel GILES, dec'd. March 1811. Buyers: Hannah Giles, Eli Giles.

Page 86
Inventory of estate of EDWARD OGLESBY, dec'd. 4 October 1810, by James Martin.

Inventory of estate of Bryant GARDNER, dec'd. March 1811. Plantation rented, 4 negroes hired; boarding William Gardner, Martin Gardner.

Page 87
Settlement of estate of James HAW, dec'd., by Catherine Haw, admr.

Settlement of estate of William BRACKEN, dec'd., Decemter 1810, by James Bracken, admr.

Page 88 — MARCH TERM 1811
Inventory of estate of JULIAS FRYETT, by Thomas Wilson, her guardian. Received of estate of William Cochran, dec'd. estate for use of Julia Fryett March Sessions 1809: two negroes' hire.

Page 89
Sale of estate of JAMES C. ALDERSON, dec'd. Buyers: James Alderson, William Alderson, Jane Alderson, Josiah Alderson. By John Polk.

Page 90
Inventory of estate of JOHN HAILS, dec'd., by David Barrett, admr.

Page 91
Account of sales of WILLIAM PHIPPS' estate, dec'd. Sold 5 July 1810, by Isaac Baker, exec. (buyers not listed)

Page 92
Inventory of estate of WILLIAM CAGE, dec'd., left in possession of Reuben Cage by will of Col. William Cage, dec'd. 16 April 1811, by R. Cage, exec.

Page 93
Sale of estate of JOHN HAIL, dec'd. (buyers and admr not listed)

Page 94
Inventory of estate of RUTH OZBROOKS, dec'd. "rent of the place for 1810: $14.25." by William Granger.

Settlement with John Parsons, admr of JAMES WILSON, dec'd.

Inventory of estate of LEWIS JONES, dec'd. September 1811, "who died in Dixon Cty., 23 October 1807." "one horse retained by the widow Rachel Jones, now Rachel Dinning, valued $45.00." by Rachel Dinning, late wife and relict of Lewis Jones, dec'd.

Page 95
Inventory of estate of ROBERT ANDERSON, dec'd., by John Anderson and John C. Gowdy.

Page 96
Inventory of estate of GREEN WILLIFORD, dec'd. 12 September 1811, by Samuel Alley.

Settlement with exec. of RUTH OZBROOKS, dec'd., William Granger, exec.

Inventory of estate of DANIEL MELTON, dec'd. by William Melton, exec.

Page 97
Inventory of estate of JAMES REED, dec'd. by Thomas Reed, exec.

Page 98
Sale of estate of JAMES REED, dec'd. Buyers: Thomas Reed, widow, "Thomas Reed for Elizabeth."

Page 101   SEPTEMBER TERM 1811
Settlement with admr. of JAMES WILSON, dec'd. September 1811, Jacob Houdeshell and Zacharius Wilson, Jr., admrs. "....by James Hodges, receipt, a legatee: $12.00."

Page 102
Settlement with exec. of JOHN SEAWELL, dec'd. by J. Cryer and Edward Sanders.

Page 104
Settlement with admrs. of WILLIAM MCCLELLAND, dec'd., William Simpson and John Sloan, admrs.

Page 105   DECEMBER TERM 1811
Sale of estate of GREEN WILLIFORD, dec'd., 10 October 1811, Buyers: Lucy Williford.

Page 106
Inventory of estate of AMBROSE TRUMBO, dec'd. by George Trumbo.

Supplemental inventory of GREEN WILLIFORD, by Samuel Alley.

Inventory of estate of HARRIS E. FARR, dec'd., by George Roberts, admr.

Page 107
Inventory of estate of MILDRED BYRUM, dec'd., by Robert Collier, admr. 26 October 1811.

Inventory of estate of JOHN HARPER, dec'd.

Supplemental Inventory of estate of LEWIS JONES, dec'd., by John Dinning and Rachel Dinning.

Page 108
Appraisement of personal property of LEWIS JONES, dec'd.

Page 109
Sale of estate of LEWIS JONES, dec'd, by John Dinning, admr.

Page 110
Sale of estate of ROBERT ANDERSON, dec'd. Buyers: John Anderson, Jr., Polly Anderson, Catharine Anderson, Robert Anderson, Peggy Anderson. By John Anderson and John C. Goudy.

MARCH TERM 1812

Page 111
Inventory of William COWDEN, dec'd., by James Cowden and John Maxey.

Inventory of James LAUDERDALE, dec'd. 220 acres, 5 negroes, note on John Lauderdale. by Samuel D. Lauderdale and Jonah Lauderdale.

Page 112
Inventory of Margaret RICHARDSON, dec'd. by William Parr, admr.

Property of orphans of Bryant GARDNER, dec'd. for 1811: one plantation and four negroes; expenses for clothing Sally Gardner, Betsy Gardner and Martin Gardner.

Page 113
Inventory of John Madewell NESBET, dec'd., September 20, 1811. by Jeane Nesbit and James Johnson.

Inventory of estate of Benjamin Williams, dec'd. 100 acres. by William Lamberth and Polly Williams.

Page 114
Inventory of estate of William BOYLE, dec'd. 25 February 1812. 10 negroes.

Page 115
Inventory of estate of William DODSON, dec'd. 1 January 1812. by Edward Sanders, admr. 13 slaves. By William Weir and Hubbard Sanders.

Page 116
Inventory of estate of Nathaniel PARKER, Sr., dec'd. by Thomas Parker and Isaac P. Parker, exrs. 13 slaves.

Page 117
Sale of estate of Margaret RICHARDSON. 28 December 1811. by William Parr, admr.

Inventory of Isaac LINDSEY, dec'd., by Isaac Lindsey and Lewis Crane, exrs.

Page 118-119
Sale of estate of John Harper, dec'd. 3 January 1817. Buyers: ...Margaret Harper, Anny Harper, Andrew Harper, Asa Harper, James Harper.

Page 120
Sale of estate of Harris E. FARR, dec'd. 10 February 1812, by George Roberts, admr.

Page 121-122
Sale of estate of William DODSON, dec'd. 20 February 1812. Buyers:....Mrs. Caty Dodson.

Page 123
Settlement with admrs. of William BROWN, dec'd., William Dorris and Mary Brown, admrs.

Page 124
Sale of estate of Miland BYRUM, dec'd. 7 January 1812. by Robert Collier.

Page 125
Commissioners appointed to divide property of James WILSON, dec'd. between heirs. The negro property--seven negroes--divided amongst nine legatees, each entitled to $234.68; to Samuel Patton, James R. Wilson, Ellen J. P. Wilson $234.68; to Zacheus Wilson, Fanny Wilson, $9.68 each. (sums held by legatees over and above their respective sums")

Inventory of estate of John NETTLES, dec'd., by John Lauderdale.

Page 126
Settlement with admrs. of estate of Alexander KIRKPATRICK, dec'd. James Kirkpatrick and Hugh Kirkpatrick, admrs.

Page 127
Settlement with guardian of George HOUSE. James Cryer, gdn. Baliss House, dec'd., James Cryer, admr. Hire of negroes for 1807-1810.

Page 128
Sale of John NESBIT, dec'd. Buyers: Jeane Nesbit, widow Nesbet, Agnes Nesbett.

Page 129
Inventory of estate of James CARUTHERS, by Hugh Caruthers and Jane Caruthers.

Page 130
Inventory of estate of Thomas PARKER, dec'd., by Judith Parker, exec.

Page 131
Inventory of estate of Robert LATIMER, by Hugh Latimer and Lucinda Latimer, execs. 348 acres.

Sale of estate of James CAROTHERS, dec'd. Buyers: H. Carothers, Jane Carothers. by Hugh Carothers and Jane Carothers.

Page 132
Sale of estate of Nathaniel PARKER, Sr., dec'd. Buyers: Robert Parker, Isaac Parker, Richard Parker, Nathaniel Parker, Thomas Parker. by Thomas Parker and Isaac P. Parker.

Page 133
Sale of estate of Thomas PARKER, dec'd. Buyers: Judith Parker. by Judith Parker, extrix.

Page 134
Inventory of hire of negroes of estate of William COCHRAN, dec'd. Negroes hired to Josiah Strange, M(W?) Stone, M. Burford, John Hubbard. by John Cochran.

Settlement with admr of Daniel SANDERS, dec'd. James Sanders, admr. "William Sanders received as guardian for one of the legatees, viz: William Sanders. Hillery Malone rec'd as gdn. for Peter Sanders, one of the legatees."

Page 135   JUNE TERM 1812
Settlement with exc. of Elias MORRISON, dec'd., James Stuard, excr.

Supplemental account of sales of estate of Mildred BYRUM, dec'd. by Robert Collier, admr.

Sale of estate of Edward OGLESBY, dec'd. 1 April 1811, by James Martin.

Page 136　　　　　　　　　　　　　　SEPTEMBER TERM 1812
Sale of estate of William COWDEN, dec'd. Buyers: James Cowden, Josiah Cowden, William Cowden, Elizabeth Cowden. by John Maxey.

Page 137
Inventory of estate of William SNODDY, dec'd. 13 May 1812. 1 negro. by Samuel Barr and David Snoddy.

Page 138
Inventory of estate of James MARKHAM, dec'd., by Samuel Gibson, admr.

Inventory of estate of William GLASGOW, dec'd. 206 acres, 1 negro. by William L. Alexander.

Supplemental inventory of estate of William PHIPPS, Sr., dec'd. by Isaac Baker, exec.

Page 139
Inventory of James DOUGLASS, dec'd., by W. Douglass.

Supplemental inventory of Isaac LINDSEY, dec'd. "an inventory of money received of William H. Douglass, belonging to the estate of Isaac Lindsey, dec'd., the amount received - $7.00; also a bond on Joshua Hadley for a quit claim deed to said Lindsey, dec'd. for 800 acres. by Lewis Crane.

Inventory of estate of Robert CAROTHERS, dec'd. 6 June 1812 by David Wilson and Hugh Carothers.

Sale of estate of Robert Carothers, dec'd. Buyers: William Carothers, Thomas Carothers, Margret Carothers, Sally Carothers, Ezekiel Carothers. by David Wilson and Hugh Carothers.

Page 140
Settlement with admrs. of William BRIGGANCE, dec'd. James Briggance, admr., and Elizabeth Briggance, admrx. Cash paid out to John Briggance, William Briggance, George S. Briggance, Catherine Briggance, Elizabeth Briggance ((and to many other persons, so is not a division.))

Page 141-142　　　　　　　　　　　　DECEMBER TERM 1812
Inventory of estate of William REED, dec'd. 100 acres. August 19, 1812. by Henry Reed and Thomas Reed.

Account of sale of estate of William REED. 5 October 1812.

Page 143-4
Sale of estate of William GLASGOW, dec'd. by William L. Alexander, admr.

Page 145
Sale of estate of James MARCUM. 27 November 1812. Buyers: Sabrinai Markham, Jasper Markham, Pleasant M. Markham.

Page 146
Supplemental inventory of estate of Nathaniel PARKER, dec'd. by Thomas Parker and Isaac Parker.

Supplemental inventory of estate of Samuel ARMSTRONG. Cash received for 231½ acres sold pursuant to will of dec'd.- $703.00. by Abel Brandon.

Page 147   APRIL TERM 1813
Settlement of estate of George DUTY, by George Gillespie and Eliza Duty, admrs. Amt paid assignee of Jabus Duty, William Duty agent for Richard Adkerson. 15 September 1812.

Supplemental inventory of estate of Zacheus Wilson, dec'd.

Page 148
Inventory of estate of DAVIS KING, dec'd. 7 March 1813, by Richard King.

Report of property of orphans of Bryant GARDNER, dec'd., 1812: land and negroes rented; tuition and boarding fees. by Martin Gardner.

Page 149
Inventory of estate of Ezekiel LINDSEY, dec'd., 20 December 1812, by Jeremiah Stark, Hubbard Saunders.

Page 150-151
Sale of estate of William SNODDY, dec'd. Among buyers: William Snoddy, David Snoddy. By Samuel Barr and David Snoddy.

Inventory of estate of Absalom CLOAR, dec'd. 12 April 1813. 225 acres lying on Otter Fork of Bledsoe's Creek in Sumner Cty.; one negro; notes on........and on John Cloar for $19.00 which is never to be called for if said John Cloar never returns from the army. By John Hubert.

Schedule of property of heirs of James HAW, dec'd. for 1808-1812. Accounting of hire of negroes; expenses for keeping, schooling and so forth four children, minors and heirs to the estate. Keeping Samuel Haw 3 years 11 months: $45.00; keeping Nancy Haw 4 months: $16.00; boarding and clothing and schooling Uriel Haw and James P. Kelly Haw 5 years: $70.00. Cash paid for running out and dividing the land belonging to said legatees. By Ephraim Garrettson, Caty X Garrettson, guardians for orphans of James Haw, dec'd.

Page 152
Appraisement of negro estate of Zacheus WILSON, dec'd. Two slaves.

Supplemental inventory of estate of William SNODDY, dec'd. 13 April 1813, by Samuel Barr and David Snoddy, executors.

Settlement of estate of John JOSEY, dec'd., by Edward Douglass, administrator. Credits: Judgement in Sumner Circuit Court: Allen Josey vs estate of John Josey, dec'd.

Page 153   JULY TERM 1813
Settlement of estate of Samuel ARMSTRONG, dec'd., by James Winchester and William Seawell, executors. Commissioners: James Weathered and John Lauderdale.

Sale of estate of Davis KING, dec'd., 4 May 1813, by Richard King, administrator.

Page 154
Appraisement of estate of Davis KING, dec'd. Note on William M. King.

Inventory of property of Richard STROTHER, dec'd. One negro. By James Strother, John McConnell.

Page 155
Inventory of estate of Basil TRAIL, dec'd. Two slaves. By Jesse Sheen and Henry Belote.

Inventory of estate of Theophilus REDDITT, dec'd. Eight negroes. By James Blakemore, administrator.

Supplemental inventory of estate of Richard TAYLOR, dec'd. 100 acres to be sold by executors expressed in last will of said Taylor and sold for $660.00 by G. D. Blakemore, executor.

Page 156   JULY TERM 1813
Sale of estate of Absalom CLOAR, dec'd., 7 May 1813. Buyers: William Cloar, Elijah Cloar, John Cloar, John Cloar, Sr. By John Hubert, executor.

Page 157
Settlement of estate of James WILSON, a lunatic, by Jacob Houdeshell, guardian.

Settlement of estate of Richard Taylor, dec'd. by George D. Blakemore and Zacheus Wilson.

Page 158
Settlement of estate of Zacheus WILSON, dec'd., by admr.

Supplemental Inventory of estate of Laban BENTHAL, dec'd., by James Cryer, Administrator. Cash rec'd. in North Carolina as a legacy due from the estate of Cloar Turner to the heirs of Laban Benthall, dec'd. Cash for hire of negroes.

Settlement of estate of Nathaniel GILES, dec'd., by John Sloan and Hannah Giles, Administrators.

Page 159   OCTOBER TERM 1813
Inventory of estate of Lunsford PITTS, dec'd. 9 August 1813, by Charles Featherston.

Page 160
Inventory of estate of Stephen PITT, dec'd. 26July 1813. By Henry Pitt and James Gambling.

Inventory of estate of John COOPER, dec'd. October 1813, at Bledsoe's Creek. 6negroes. By John Cooper, executor.

Inventory of estate of Nancy GRAHAM, dec'd, by Nelly Graham, executrix. One negro.

Page 161
Sale of estate of John COOPER, dec'd. Buyers: John Cooper, Franky Cooper, Peurify Cooper. By John Cooper, executor.

Sale of estate of Richard STROTHER, dec'd. 7 August 1813. Buyers: James Strother. By James Strother and John McConnell, executors.

Sale of estate of John NETTLES, dec'd.

Inventory of estate of Isaac LINDSEY, dec'd., by Isaac Lindsey and Lewis Crane, executors.

Page 162
Settlement of estate of James REED, dec'd., by Thomas Reed, executor. Cash paid out to Hannah Reed, William Reed, John Reed, Elizabeth Reed. Sale of land: $1,037.63, by John Barr and Elijah Simpson.

Settlement of estate of orphans of James WILSON, dec'd. by John Parsons, guardian.

Page 163　　　　　　　　　　　　　　　　　FEBRUARY TERM 1814
Settlement of estate of Samuel WHITWORTH, by Will Trigg, Jr., guardian.

Inventories of estates of John ORR and Frances ORR, dec'd. 6 January 1814, by James Alderson and John Boyle.

Supplemental inventory of Lunsford PITTS, dec'd. 1 November 1813, by Charles Featherston, executor.

Page 164
Division of negro estate of Charles ELLIOTT, dec'd among his heirs, agreeable to order of court October Term 1813 as follows: negroes to Learner Blackman, Mireah Elliott. 28 January 1814.

Inventory of estate of Moses YOUNG, dec'd., by Josiah G. Giles, administrator.

Page 165
Inventory of estate of Jane Carothers, dec'd. 7 February 1814, byJonathan Wilson and Hugh Carothers.

Inventory of estate of William OGLES, dec'd. 24 February 1814, by John Givin.

Page 166
Sale of estate of Lunsford PITTS, dec'd. 2 November 1816, by Charles Featherston, executor.

Page 167
Inventory of and sale of negores of estate of James HAW, dec'd. Jesse Joyner, guardian of heirs of said dec'd. 1 slave sold to Nancy Haw, 1 slave sold to James Kirkpatrick, 1 slave sold to William Jones.

Page 168
Inventory of estate of William M. KING, dec'd. One slave. Note on Samuel King. By Richard King and James Hassell, administrators.

Inventory of estate of Hugh ROGAN, dec'd, by W. Hall, administrator. Six slaves.

Page 169
Inventory of heirs of Bryant Gardner, dec'd. For 1813: expenditures for Martin Gardner, Betsey Gardner, and Sally Gardner. By Isaac Walton, guardian.

Page 170
Settlement of estate of John MAXWELL NESBITT, dec'd, by James Johnston and James Nesbitt, administrators.

Settlement of estate of Isaac LINDSEY, dec'd, by executor. 19 October 1813.

Page 171
Settlement of estate of Charles ELLIOTT, dec'd. by administrators.

Settlement of estate of Lewis JONES, dec'd., by John Dinning, administrator.

Settlement of estate of Laban BENTHALL, dec'd., by admr. July 1813. Hire of negroes.

Page 172*   MAY TERM 1814
Settlement of estate of Margaret RICHARDSON, dec'd., by William Parr, admr.

Sale of estate of William OGLE, dec'd. Buyers: Peggy Ogles. By John Gwin.

Page 173
Inventory of John ANDERSON, dec'd., by William B. Anderson and John C. Goudy, admrs.

Inventory of estate of Thomas SPARKMAN, dec'd., by Isaac Walton, admr.

Inventory of estate of Larkin BRADFORD, dec'd. Note on William Bradford. By Isaac Baker, admr.

Inventory of estate of James HOLLIS, dec'd. One slave. By Jesse Hollis.

Page 174-5
Inventory of estate of Maria ELLIOTT, orphan of Charles ELLIOTT, dec'd. by Learner Blackman, guardian. Five slaves. 108 acres.

Sale of estate of Jane CAROTHERS, dec'd., by Hugh Carothers and Jonathan Wilson, execrs. 15 March 1814. Buyers: Hugh Carothers, Ezekiel Carothers, Thomas Carothers.

Page 176
Sale of estate of Hugh ROGAN, dec'd. 26 March 1814. Buyers: Nancy Rogan, Frances Rogan. By William Hall.

Page 177
Settlement of estate of Samuel Armstrong, dec'd., by Able Brandon and John Knox, execrs. ".....and the only part of the property remaining unsold is a tract of land lying in State of North Carolina."

* See last page for omitted data on KING.

Settlement of estate of John NETTLES, dec'd, by John Lauderdale, admr.

Page 178
Settlement of estate of James C. ALDERSON, dec'd, by admrs.

Allotment to widow and family of Moses YOUNG, dec'd. 28 May 1814.

Page 179
Allotment of dower to Eliza DUTY, widow of George DUTY, dec'd. Dower in tract of land on which she now lives, bds Bledsoe's Creek: 50 acres, and her right of dower in negro property $248.50, leaving balance due from said Eliza to her six children $41.43. 29 March 1814.

Page 180
Sale of estate of Moses YOUNG, dec'd, by Josiah E. Giles, admr. Buyers: Elizabeth Young, Joseph Young.

Page 181
Sale of estate of John ORR and Frances ORR, dec'd. by James Alderson and John Boyle. 22 March 1814. Buyers: John ORR, Green B. Orr, David Orr. By James Alderson and John Boyle.

Page 182   AUGUST TERM 1814
Inventory of estate of John D. HANNA, by Martha Hanna, W. Hall, and William Hanna, executors. 12 negroes. 26 August 1814.

Page 183
Inventory of estate of William Douglass, dec'd. 17 August 1814. 490 acres in Wilson Cty, 220 acres in Montgomery Cty., 500 acres on Fall Creek in Wilson Cty., 4 negroes. By Alfred Douglass, execr.

Page 184
Inventory of estate of John STARK, dec'd. by Sarah X Stark and Thornton Stark. 13 slaves.

Inventory of estate of David BRIGGANCE, dec'd, by James Strother.

Page 185
Inventory of estate of Richard SANFORD, dec'd. By T. Sanford. 17 slaves.

Page 186
Inventory of estate of John FARR, dec'd., by Ephriam Phar. 16 June 1814.

Inventory of estate of William FELTON, dec'd. by Letty X Felton. 22 August 1814.

Inventory of estate of Thomas Swann, dec'd, by Emelia C. Swann, extrx.

Page 187
Sale of estate of John Anderson, dec'd. 25 July 1814. Buyers: Sarah Anderson, Lemma(?) Anderson, Pleasant Anderson. Sarah Anderson also bought 15 shares in Cotton Factory. By J. C. Goudy and William B. Anderson, admrs.

Page 188
Inventory of estate of Daniel JONES, dec'd, by Elizabeth Jones. Three negroes. Also Sale; buyers: Elizabeth Jones.

Page 189
Year's Provision to widow of Daniel JONES, de'cd. who died 24 April 1814. 4 June 1814.

Sale of estate of John ORR and Frances ORR, dec'd., by John Boyle, admr. To Elizabeth Snoddy: 61 acres sold by consent.

Inventory of estate of Henry BARNS, dec'd. 26 August 1814, by John Cotton.

Settlement of estate of Robett HARRIS, dec'd, by Greenberry Orr and Blair Harris, exrs. Cash paid to Martha Harris, Mary G. Harris, Martha S. Harris, and Elizabeth Harris, Blair Harris. Balance due from settlement previous to 22 December 1809.

Page 190
Inventory of estate of Robert HARRIS, dec'd. continued. Cash rec'd of Nicholas Young - Virginia: $748.75.

Page 191
Settlement of estate of Nathaniel Parker, dec'd, by Thomas J. Parker, exr. Cash paid to Thomas Parker, Isaac Parker, Robert Parker, Nathaniel Parker, JohnParker, and others.

Page 192   NOVEMBER TERM 1814
Inventory of estate of John NORRIS, dec'd., by Thomas Blakemore, William Norris. Five negroes.

Inventory of estate of Mary Ann Granger, dec'd. 29 October 1814. Aged between 85 and 90 years; estate has notes on Absalom Goostree and Thomas Pound, both dated October 1800. By Elisha Barnard.

Page 193
Inventory of estate of William EDWARDS, dec'd. by William Edwards, Jr., exec.

Inventory of estate of Ezekiel NORMAN, dec'd., by Febe Norman.

Inventory of estate of David G. ROBERTSON, dec'd. by William Robertson, admr.

Page 194
Inventory of estate of Colin ADAMS, dec'd. 22 August 1814. 19 negroes. By William Parr, admr.

Sale of estate of David Briggance, dec'd. 17 September 1814. Buyers: Polly Briggance, Charles N. Briggance, James Briggance, Jr. By James Strother, admr.

Page 195
Inventory of estate of Thomas GROVES, dec'd., by Thomas Groves and Allen Groves. 590 acres, 8 negroes.

Page 196
Inventory of estate of Thomas T. CULBERT, dec'd. Partner in firm of Crockett and Culbert. By George Crockett.

Page 197-201
Sale of estate of William DOUGLASS, dec'd., by Alfred Douglass, exec. Buyers: Alfred Douglass, Peggy Douglass, Jesse Douglass, John H. Douglass, Edward Douglass.

Settlement of estate of William HAMILTON, dec'd., by William Douglass, late exec. Hire of negro girl.

Sale of estate of Henry Barnes, dec'd., by John Cotten.

Inventory of estate of David BRIGGANCE, dec'd., by James Strother, admr.

Page 202
Settlement of estate of Moses CUMMINGS, dec'd.

Page 203   FEBRUARY TERM 1815
Inventory of estate of George LOGAN, dec'd., by W. Hall, exec.

Page 204
Sale of estate of Ezekiel NORMAN, dec'd. Buyers: Phebe Norman. By Phebe Norman.

Inventory of estate of John F. CARR, dec'd. By King Carr.

Page 205
Inventory of estate of Samuel WILSON, dec'd. List of property willed to Sarah Wilson, wife of Samuel Wilson, dec'd. One negro woman and child to James C. Wilson. By Israel Moore and Jonathan Wilson, execs.

Inventory of estate of Benjamin H. STUBBLEFIELD, dec'd., by William Stubblefield, admr.

Inventory of estate of William FELTON, dec'd., by Lettitia Felton, admr.

Page 206
Sale of estate of Collin ADAMS, dec'd., by William Parr, admr.

Page 207
Inventory of estate of heirs of Samuel ARMSTRONG, dec'd. by John Gillispie, guardian for said heirs. Expenses for schooling of Peggy Adams, Zenos Adams, Knox(?) Adams, Samuel Adams.

Page 208-210
Inventory of estate of heirs of Bryant GARDNER, dec'd., by Isaac Walton, guardian. Plantation rented to Isaac Walton. Expenses: Boarding Martin Gardner, orphan, and schooling.

Sale of estate of Thomas T. CULBERT, dec'd. Accounting of property belonging to firm of Crockett and Culbert. By George Crockett, A. D. M., by Robert Crockett.

Page 211
Inventory of estate of heirs of George DUTY, dec'd., by George Gillispie, guardian. Hire of negroes. "Widow note Debit by dividing negroes $41.43 not yet due." "Appointed guardian July term 1813."

Settlement of estate of Harris E. FARR, dec'd., by George Roberts, Admr.

Settlement of estate of Edward OGLESBY, dec'd., by James Marten, Admr. Charge against estate - 8 November 1808. Settlement date - 14 September 1812.

Supplemental inventory of estate of Nathaniel PARKER, dec'd., by Thomas Parker, andIsaac P. Parker.

Page 212   February Term 1815
Settlement with guardians of James NEELY and Alexander NEELY, orphans of JOHN NEELY, dec'd., by Isaac Bledsoe and George D. Blakemore, guardians. "...in handsof William Neely, former guardian in June 1805 - $222.79. 4 January 1815.

Settlement of estate of William GLASGOW, dec'd., by William L. Alexander, admr. 15 September 1814.

Inventory of estate of William NOEL, dec'd., by Thomas Noel, admr. 100 acres.

Page 213   MAY TERM 1815
Inventory of estate of Daniel LEGGET, dec'd., by Richard Garrison. One due bill on Whitmal Leggett - $23.00.

Supplemental Inventory of Jonathan ROGERS, dec'd.

Inventory of estate of John BOREN, dec'd., by Sarah Boren, Admr. 137 acres.

Page 214-215
Inventory of estate of William B. ANTHONY, dec'd., by Susan Anthony. Nine male slaves and eight female slaves, with dates of birth;...."one rifle gun which Mr. Bandy says Mr. Anthony directed it to be given to his son Albert"....
"Robert Bruce owes the estate $7.65;money in the hands of John Austin of Hanover County, Virginia about $60.00"....
money in the hands of Mark Anthony of Bedford County, Virginia."
Notes due estate.....John A. Anthony.

Page 216

Inventory of estate of James LAUDERDALE, dec'd., by John Hawkins andJohn Lauderdale. One slave.

Inventory of estate of Staunton ROGERS, dec'd. 80 acres.

Page 217

Inventory of estate of Jonathan ROGERS, dec'd. 100 acres. by Henry Vinson and William McAdams.

Inventory of estate of David PHILIPS, dec'd., by Patsy Philips, admr.

Inventory of estate of Joel BOYKEN, dec'd., by James Boyken. "...pay as a soldier under Capt. Neal."

Page 218-219

Account of sales of estate of George LOGAN, dec'd., by William Hall, exec. Buyers.....Mrs. E. Logan, John Lauderdale.

Sale of estate of Mary Anne GRAINGER, dec'd., 24 December 1814, by Elisha Barnard, Admr.

Page 220

Inventory of estate of Lamuel BOYKIN, dec'd., byMildred Boykin. 500 acres.

Inventory of estate of William HALL, dec'd., by Elizabeth Hall. Note on Robert Hall dated 4 October 1810....for $25.00.

Inventory of estate of Bartemeus BRUCE, by Jacob Harder, Admr. "One certificate 39th U.S. Infantry for his service a balance due...for 10 months pay and travelling expenses from Fort Montgomery, Mississippi Territory to Sumner Cty., Tennessee."

Page 221

Inventory of estate of Jeremiah HAIL, dec'd., by Richard Carr, admr.

Inventoryof estate of Robert GARDNER, dec'd., by Jane Gardner.

Inventory of estate of John Mitchell, dec'd....died in Battle of New Orleans, 23 December 1814...by Sol. Mitchell.

Supplemental inventory of estate of Jane CARUTHERS, dec'd., by Hugh Caruthers and Jonathan Wilson, execs.

Settlement of estate of Davis KING, dec'd., by Richard King, Admr.

Page 222

Inventory of estate of Samuel WILSON, dec'd., by Israel Moore and Jonathan Wilson, extrs. Aomng buyers....Samuel Wilson, James C. Wilson, Sarah Wilson, Zacheus Wilson, John Wilson. Two slaves.

Settlement of estate of Solomon RUYLE, by Hugh McBride, Admr. Charge against estate - 29 August 1814.

Page 223   AUGUST TERM 1815

Inventory of estate of Norman PEEK, dec'd., by James McKindree and Joshua Smith, Extrs. 320 acres, 110 acres, and 30 acres.

Inventory of estate of Samuel LUNSFORD, dec'd., by Susanna Lunsford.

Page 224

Inventory of estate of Jasper Markum, dec'd., by R. Perry. 33 acres.

Inventory of estate of Terrisha STOVALL, dec'd., by W. Stovall. Six slaves.

Page 225

Inventory of estate of Abram BLEDSOE, dec'd., by Isaac Bledsoe, Henry Bledsoe, James Weathered, and Milly Bledsoe, Extrs. Ten slaves.

Page 226

Inventory of estate of Alexander MCMILLAN, dec'd., by Christine McMillan, Admr.

Inventory of estate of James Cauldwell, dec'd., by Hardy Cauldwell, Admr. "Two dollars 80 cents due on George Sarver for sale of clothes...due from U.S. wages for six months tour in themilitia."

Inventory of estate of Henry BRADFORD, dec'd., by H. C. Bradford. One slave.

Inventory of estate of Garlan YANCY, dec'd., by Robert H. Yancy, Admr.

Page 227

Inventory of estate of Joseph MCDANIEL, dec'd., by William Parr, Admr. Notes on Andrew McDaniel and Stephen McDaniel.

Inventory of estate of Edmund Jones, dec'd, by Needham Green. "Pay as a militia soldier six months and twenty-one days."

Inventory of estate of Henry BLOODWORTH, dec'd., by Dolly Bloodworth.

Page 228

Inventory of estate of Allen ROBERTSON, dec'd., by Anna Robertson, Philip Day. "...his wages for a tour duty one month and 21 days."

Inventory of estate of Stephen WINCHESTER, dec'd., by J. Winchester and George Roberts.

Inventory of estate of West EDWARDS, dec'd., by Thomas F. Edwards, Admr. Three slaves.

Page 229

Account of sale of estate of William B. ANTHONY, dec'd., by Susan Anthony, admr.

Sale of estate of Jonathan ROGERS, dec'd., by Griswold Latimer, Admr. 10 June 1815. Among buyers: Ruth Rogers, Samuel Rogers.

Page 230

Inventory of estate of Isaac DAY, dec'd., by Philip Day.

Inventory of estate of Thomas NEEL, dec'd., by John Dobbins. Four slaves; unwritten note of John Dobbins for negro girl acknowledged.

Inventory of estate of William BOON, dec'd., by Henry Hardy, Admr.

Page 231

Inventory of estate of Elizabeth KETTLE, dec'd., by Jacob Strator, Admr.

Sale of estate of William HALL, dec'd., by Elizabeth Hall, Admr. Among buyers: Elizabeth Hall, Michael Green, Cradick H. May.

Page 232

Sale of estate of Staunton ROGERS, dec'd., 10 June 1815, by Samuel Rogers, Griswold Latimer, Admrs. Among buyers: Lucretia Rogers, Elizabeth Rogers, Jonathan Latimer, Samuel Rogers, Hannah Rogers, Ruth Rogers.

Page 233

Inventory of estate of William HENDERSON, dec'd., 12 July 1815, by John Henderson, John Henson. "Six months and twenty days in the United States service."

Inventory of estate of James MALLARD, dec'd., by Joseph Matt. "...a claim for a tour of militia service under General Jackson in the south."

Inventory of estate of George TILLY, dec'd., by Charity Tilly. "...a discharge for three months five days for driver as a private performed under General Carroll."

Inventory of the estate of Isaac Forrest, dec'd., by Elisha Green, Admr.

Sale of estate of William NOEL, dec'd., by Thomas Noel, Admr.

Page 234

Settlement of estate of Mary Ann GRAINGER, dec'd. Sale of estate on 24 December 1814. "...to her boarding from year 1808 July until the 29th of October 1814 - $207.50. by Elisha Barnard 28 June 1815.

Page 235

Settlement of estate of William OGEL, dec'd., by John Given, admr.

Year's allowance for widow and family of William HALL, dec'd., 10 June 1815.

Year's allowance for widow and family of David Philips, dec'd. 10 June 1815.

Year's allowance for family of Joseph MCDANIEL.

Page 236   NOVEMBER TERM 1815

Settlement of estate of Daniel JONES, dec'd., 10 June 1815.

Inventory of estate of James CHAPMAN, dec'd., by Benjamin Chapman and John Chapman, admrs. Book accounts on Samuel Chapman, 10 February 1810 and 25 November 1811, and on Philip Chapman, 11 September 1813.

Page 237-238

Inventory and sale of estate of Stephen WINCHESTER, dec'd., by J. Winchester, George Roberts, extrs.

Sale of estate of Thomas NEALE, dec'd., 29 September 1815, by John Dobbins, Admr. Among buyers: Jane Neale, B. Neale, Henry Neale, Samuel Neale, James Neale.

Sale of estate of Abram BLEDSOE, dec'd., 15 June 1815, by Isaac Bledsoe, Henry R. Bledsoe, James Weathered, Milly Bledsoe, extrs.

Page 239

Supplemental sale of estate of Abram Bledsoe, dec'd., by Isaac Bledsoe, Henry R. Bledsoe, James Weathered, Milly Bledsoe, extrs., 26 October 1815. "....residence: Bledsoe Creek."

Page 240

Sale of estate of William HENDERSON, dec'd., by John Henderson, "one of the admrs." Among Buyers: Patsey Henderson, Thomas Henderson, John Henderson.

Inventory of estate of Basil TRAIL, dec'd., by Elizabeth Trail, Admr. "...discharge of four months and thirty days."

Page 241

Year's allowance for widow Patsy Henderson and family of William HENDERSON, dec'd.

Year's allowance for widow Susanna LUNSFORD and family of Samuel LUNSFORD, dec'd.

Inventory of estate of Robert MCCRILLES, dec'd., by J. W. Byrn, Admr.

Inventory of estate of Harris AVENT, dec'd., by J. W. Byrn, Admr.

Inventory of estate of Willie THOMAS, dec'd., by Thomas Barrett. "...to his discharge for a tour of duty for six months at New Orleans."

Page 242-243

Sale of estate of James CALDWELL, dec'd., 16 September 1815, by Hardy Caldwell, Admr.

Settlement of estate of Robert ANDERSON, dec'd.; notes due estate by Catherine Anderson 2 October 1812, John C. Goudy, Polly Anderson, Robert Anderson; vouchers: William B. Anderson.

Settlement of estate of Lunsford PITTS, dec'd., by Charles Featherstone, Extr., 21 September 1815.

Page 244

Inventory of estate of Rev. Learner BLACKMAN, dec'd., by George Elliott. Five slaves.

Sale of estate of Elizabeth KETTLES, dec'd., by Jacob Strator.

Page 245

Sale of estate of Joseph MCDANIEL, dec'd., by William Parr, Admr.

Inventory of estate of Joel BROWN, dec'd., by James Brown.

Page 246

Inventory of estate of Mary Ann GARDNER, dec'd. One slave.

Inventory of estate of James KENNEDY, dec'd., by E. Cates.

Sale of estate of Allen ROBERTSON, dec'd., 20 September 1815, by Ann Robertson and Philip Day, admrs.

Sale of estate of Isaac DAY, dec'd., 20 September 1815, by **Philip Day, Admr.**

Sale of estate of George Tilly, dec'd., 14 September 1815, by Charity Tilly.

Page 247

Inventory of estate of Asa Beshears, Julia Beshears, and Jeney BESHEARS, by their guardian Silas Polk. Four slaves.

Supplemental Inventory of estate of Larken BRADFORD, dec'd., by Isaac Baker, Admr.

Sale of estate of Larken Bradford, dec'd., by Isaac Baker.

Inventory of estate of Jonathan Peairs, dec'd., by Karin Happet Peairs, Admr. Six Slaves.

Page 248   FEBRUARY TERM 1816

Inventory of estate of William MCGRADY, dec'd., by John McGrady.

Inventory of estate of Rowland HOOD, dec'd., by Mary Hood.

Page 249
Inventory of estate of Thomas NORRIS, dec'd., by William Norris, Admr. 100 acres "on ridge in Smith County, TN;" one note on Samuel Norris.

Inventory of estate of Enos King, dec'd., a man of colour, by William H. Anderson.

Inventory of estate of Esther LOGAN, dec'd., by W. Hall, Admr.

Page 250

Inventory of estate of Porter ALLEN, dec'd., by Will Trigg, Jr. Shoemaker tools.

Inventory of estate of Adam CRUMP, dec'd., by Will Trigg, Jr.

Inventory of estate of John HARRIS, dec'd., by Thomas Scurry.

Page 251

Inventory of estate of John HARGROVE, dec'd., by Thomas Preston. Nine slaves.

Inventory of estate of William POE, dec'd., by Elizabeth Poe.

Sale of estate of Learner BLACKMAN, dec'd., 23 January 1816, by George Elliott. Among buyers: Mrs. Blackman.

Page 252

Sale of estate of Mary Ann Gardner, dec'd., by John Sloan, Extr. One slave. Among buyers: Joshua Bradley, Blair Harris.

Sale of estate of Garland YANCY, dec'd., by Robert H. Yancy. Among buyers: Polly Yancy, Robert Yancy, Tyry Yancy.

Page 253-254

Sale of estate of Robert Gardner, dec'd., by Jane Gardner, Admr. Among buyers: Jane Gardner, Betsy Gardner, Polly Gardner.

Sale of estate of Stephen PITT, dec'd., 6 November 1813, by James Gambling. Among buyers: Nancy Pitt, Henry Pitt, Davis Pitt, Robert Pitt, Joseph Pitt.

Page 255

Sale of estate of Esther LOGAN, dec'd, by W. Hall, Extr. Also "return of the sale of 111 acres...the property of the heirs of George LOGAN, dec'd., lying on Rocky Creek," 14 December 1815.

Year's allowance to the widow and family of Enos KING, dec'd.

Page 256

Inventory of estate of Moriah ELLIOTT, daughter of Charles ELLIOTT, dec'd., by Elizabeth Blackman, guardian. Six slaves.

Inventory of estate of heirs of Samuel ARMSTRONG, dec'd., by John Gillespie, gdn. Acct. of expenditures: August 1815 Margaret's expense for clothing, Knoxes tuition, Zenos and Samuel's books and tuition.

Inventory of estate of heirs of George DUTY, dec'd., by George Gillespie, gdn. "for 1814-1815".

Sale of estate of Col. James LAUDERDALE, dec'd., by John Hawkins and John Lauderdale, Admrs.

Sale of estate of Willie THOMAS, dec'd., by Thomas Barrett, Admr. 13 January 1816.

Page 257

Settlement of estate of John and Frances ORR, dec'd. "Voucher proved by Greenberry Orr against John Orr," Voucher #2 paid to Greenberry Orr; Voucher #12 laid in by John Orr."

Supplemental Settlement of estate of William MCCELLAND, dec'd., by John Barr, Elijah Simpson.

Page 258   MAY TERM 1816

Inventory of estate of Joseph MOTHERAL, dec'd., by Joseph Orr and William Glover, Extrs. Five slaves.

Page 259-262

Inventory of estate of Thomas WINN, dec'd., by John Hurley, Admr. Note on Mourning Winn.

Sale of estate of Thomas WINN, dec'd. 12 March 1816. One slave. Among buyers: John Hurley, William Hurley. By John Hurley, Admr.

Sale of powdermill of Thomas WINN, dec'd., by J. Hurley, Admr.

Page 263

Inventory of estate of William MARTIN, dec'd., by Mathew Martin and Oliver Martin.

Inventory of estate of Andrew CLARK, dec'd., by James Wilson.

Inventory of estate of Samuel BUGG, dec'd., by Anselin D. Bugg. Forty-seven slaves.

Page 264

Inventory of estate of Alexander OWSLER, by James Sanders, Admr. Note on Helen Owsler. Three slaves.

Inventory of estate of David HENRY, dec'd., by Moses Henry, Samuel Henry, Admrs. One slave.

265-268

Inventory of estate of William EDWARDS, dec'd., by Elizabeth Edwards. note on Richard Edwards; 14 notes on William Beard.

Inventory of estate of James CRYER, dec'd.(many notes due estate)

269

Inventory of estate of Mourning WYNN, dec'd., by Peter Winn, Admr. 114 acres, 2 slaves.

Inventory of estate of William and Mary WARNER, dec'd., by John Sheppard.

Inventory of estate of James NORVELL, dec'd., by Jesse Sheen, Admr.

Page 270

Inventory of estate of Richard GILLESPIE, dec'd., by John Shelby, Admr.

Inventory of estate of Willie BOHANNON, dec'd., by Joseph Townsend.

Inventory of estate of William GEORGE, dec'd., by Jesse Hunt, Admr. 16 April 1816.

Page 271

Inventory of medicine of Doctor Richard GILLESPIE, dec'd.

Page 272

Inventory of estate of Robert Overstreet, dec'd.,by Jonah Crain.

Inventory of estate of Allen HOWARD, dec'd., by G. B. Howard. "...died in the campaign at Orleans on the 24th day of January 1816 under the command of Matthew Neil then Captain in the militia of infantry from Sumner County and under the command of Major General William Carroll under command of Major General Andrew Jackson.....said Allen Howard did ...serve in the 15th Regiment of Militia as a private... for two months and twelve days."

Supplemental inventory of estate of Enos KING, dec'd., by William H. Anderson, Admr. One slave.

Page 273

Inventory of estate of John BRIGANCE, dec'd. by Patsey Brigance.

Inventory of estate of Elizabeth BRIGANCE, dec'd.,by Harvey R. Willis, Admr. 28 March 1816.

Inventory of estate of Richard ERWIN, dec'd., by James Erwin. "...one discharge for two months and fourteen days."

Record of division of negro estate of Daniel BENTHALL, dec'd. Six negroes, valued at $1335.00, divided equally among four legatees."

Page 274-275

Sale of estate of John B. JOHNSON, dec'd., by E.E. Chapman Johnson, Extr., by his agent S. Hunt. 15 December 1815. One slave. Among buyers: Sion Hunt.

Inventory of estate of William CRAIN, dec'd., by Lewis Crain. Inventory of property allowed the widow for the support of the family.

Page 276

Sale of estate of Jesse WELLS, dec'd., by James McKain, Admr. 19 January 1809. One slave. Among buyers: Rebekah Wells, Henry Wells, James McKain.

Page 277

Inventory of estate of Joseph MALLARD, dec'd., by Elizabeth Mallard and David Hickison.

Supplemental inventory of estate of William REED, dec'd. by Henry Reed and Thomas Reed, Admrs.

Inventory of estate of Robert BOYKIN, dec'd., by Delilah Boykin, Admrx. 100 acres.

Page 278

Inventory of estate of Joseph George, dec'd., by David George, Admr.

Inventory of estate of Samuel STEWART, Jr., dec'd., by Israel Moore. "....some pay due him for his service in the Army."

Supplemental inventory of estate of William POE, dec'd., by Elizabeth Poe.

Inventory of estate of Thomas NEELEN, dec'd.

Page 279

Inventory of estate of Robert MOORE, dec'd., by Zachariah Green. Two slaves.

Inventory of estate of Nimrod K. BLAGG, dec'd., by Mary Blagg, admr.

Inventory of estate of John BADGET, dec'd., by Nancy Badget.

Inventory of estate of John BOYCE, dec'd., by Nancy Boyce, Admr.

Supplemental inventory of estate of Stephen WINCHESTER, dec'd., by James Winchester and George Roberts, Extrs.

Page 280

Inventory of estate of David WATSON, dec'd., by John Hall.

Supplemental inventory of estate of William M. KING, dec'd., by Richard King and Jennett Hassell, Admrs. Account on Eneas King.

Page 281

Sale of estate of Terisha STOVALL, dec'd., by William Stovall, Admr. 21 December 1815. Among buyers: Sinday Stovall, William Stovall, James Stovall, Bird Stovall, Thomas Stovall.

Page 281-282

Sale of estate of Enos KING, dec'd., by William H. Anderson, Admr.

Inventory of estate of Willis HUNLEY, dec'd., by John Hunley, Admr.

Page 283-284

Inventory of estate of John Wooten, dec'd., by William Craven. "one month and nineteen days' pay due from the United States as sergeant."

Sale of estate of Willis HUNLEY, dec'd., by John Hunley, Admr. 12 March 1816. One slave. Among buyers: William Hunley, John Hunley, William Wilks, William Hall.

Page 285-6

Sale of estate of William M. McGready, dec'd., by John McGready. 29 March 1816. Among buyers: John McGready, Margaret McGready, M. McGready, Isreal McGready.

Supplemental inventory of estate of Thomas NEEL, dec'd., by John Dobbins, and Jane Neal, Admrs.

Year's allowance for widow and family of William B. Anthony, dec'd.

Page 287

Year's allowance for widow Charity TILLY and family of George TILLEY, dec'd.

Settlement of estate of William KING, dec'd., by Richard King and Jennet Hassel, Admrs. Receipt of Priscilla King, widow; receipt of Jennett Hassell, guardian.

Settlement of estate of James MARKHAM, dec'd., by J. Winchester, Admr. Notes collected on Joseph Markham, Pleasant Markham. Note on Sabrina Markham.

Page 288

Settlement of estate of James CAROTHERS, dec'd, by Jane Carothers, and Hugh Carothers, extrs. Allowance to Hugh Carothers for boarding two children two years.

Settlement of estate of Stephen PITT, dec'd., by Henry Pitt, Admr., and Dr. James Gambling, Admr.

Page 289

Sale of estate of Hugh GOURLEY, dec'd. Among buyers: Margaret Gourley, Mary Gourley, John Gourley, Robert Gourley, James Gourley, Adam Gourley.

Inventory of estate of Joseph BARRON, dec'd.

Year's allowance for family of Jonathan PEARCE, dec'd. 10 March 1816.

Page 290   AUGUST TERM 1816

Inventory of estate of James BUSBY, dec'd., by William Busby. Eight slaves.

Inventory of estate of Nathan RICKMAN, dec'd., by Frances Rickman and Thomas Rickman, extrs.

Page 291

Supplemental inventory of estate of James CRYER, dec'd., by Hardy M. Cryer, Admr. " one discharge for seven months service performed by Isham Station as a mounted gunman in General John Coffee's Brigade."

Sale of estate of Porter Allen, dec'd., by Will Trigg, Jr., Admr. 23 March 1816.

Page 292

Sale of estate of David HENRY, dec'd., by Moses Henry and Samuel Henry, Admrs. One slave.

Page 293

Sale of estate of Jonathan Peairs, dec'd., by Karen Peairs, Admr. Among buyers: Isaac Peairs, George Peairs, William Peairs, Karen Peairs.

Inventory of estate of James HARTEN, dec'd., by John Harten, Extr. 200 acres; note on John Harten.

Supplemental inventory of estate of David HENRY, dec'd., by Moses Henry and Samuel Henry, Admrs.

Page 294

Inventory of estate of William EDWARDS, dec'd., by Elisa Edwards.

Inventory of estate of Andrew HOUGH, dec'd., by Vilot Hough.

Inventory of estate of Thomas DUREN, dec'd., by Goerge Duren.

Page 295-296

Inventory of estate of William PURVIS, dec'd., 18 April 1816. "Negro man under mortgage to Nathan Barnes."

Sale of estate of Joseph Motheral, by Joseph Robb and William Glover, Extrs. 25 July1816. Among buyers: Sarah Motheral.

Page 297

Sale of estate of Adam CRUMP, dec'd., by Will Trigg, Jr., Admr. 22 March 1816.

Page 298

Inventory of estate of John HARRIS, dec'd., by Thomas Scurry, Admr.

Sale of estate of Samuel LUNSFORD, dec'd., by Hum Bate, Admr. "Received for services at New Orleans....". Among buyers: Susanna Lunsford, Levy Lunsford.

Inventory of estate of James Watkins, dec'd., by Robert Watkins. 242 acres.

Page 299

Sale of estate of William GEORGE, dec'd., by Jesse Hunt, Admr. Among buyers: Isaac George, Lensey George.

Sale of estate of Joseph GEORGE, dec'd., by David George, Admr.

Page 300

Sale of estate of David WATSON, dec'd., byJohn Hall, Admr. June 1816. Among buyers: James Watson, Charles Watson.

Page 301

Inventory of estate of Enos BENTHALL, dec'd., by James Venson.

Inventory of estate of heirs of James McDOWELL, dec'd., by Jesse Sheen.

Inventory of estate of William PARR, dec'd., by James Walton, Admr. Thirteen slaves.

Page 302-303

Sale of estate of Joseph MALLARD, dec'd., by David S. Higgason. Among buyers: Elizabeth Mallard, Paton Stuard.

Sale of estate ofWilliam CRAIN, dec'd., by Lewis Crain, Admr.

Settlement of estate of Lunsford PITTS, dec'd., by Charles Featherstone, acting Extr. Cash paid Bunton H. Pitts balance of legacy $15.25; Cash paid Wilson Yandle $21.25; Cash paid John Yandell $22.12; Cash Paid L. C. Pitts $21.25; Cash paid Henry Pitts $21.25; Cash Paid Samuel P. Black $21.25.

Page 304

Settlement of estate of William BOON, dec'd., by Henry Hardy, Admr. Note against James Boon "pending in court."

Settlement with guardian of James House, orphan of Bailess HOUSE, dec'd., by James House, Esq., guardian. 12 June 1816. Hire of negroes accounted for from 1810-1816; legacy in cash to James House - $100.00.

Page 305

Settlement made with guardian of Bailess House, orphan, by James Cryer, guardian. Legacy in cash to Bailess House - $100.00; hire of negroes 1810-1816. 12 June 1816.

Settlement with Jesse Sheen, guardian for James and Patsy Norvil, orphans, two of the heirs of Edward NORVIL, dec'd.

Page 306

Settlement made with Jesse Sheen, guardian for the heirs of James McDOWELL, dec'd.

Inventory of estate of Elizabeth COVINGTON, dec'd., by James Barry, Admr.

Year's allowance for widow and family of David HENRY, dec'd., 18 June 1816.

Year's allowance for widow and family of Joseph MALLARD, dec'd.

Page 306

Inventory of estate of Drury STONE, dec'd., by John Hunley, Admr. Four slaves.

Page 307-308

Sale of estate of Drury Stone, dec'd., by John Hunley, Admr. 28 June 1816. Among buyers: Peter Townsend, Joseph Townsend, William Hunley, Richard Stone, John Stone.

Sale of estate of Joseph Barrow, dec'd. 24 June 1816.

Page 309   NOVEMBER TERM 1816

Sale of estate of Elizabeth BRIGANCE, dec'd., by Harvey A. Willis, Admr. 22 June 1816.

Inventory of estate of Elijah Humphreys, dec'd., by C. L. Humphreys, Extr. 26 August 1816.

Page 310

Inventory of estate of William PURVIS, dec'd., by Callen Purvis, Admr. One negro man "under a mortgage to Nathan Barns."

Sale of estate of Willie BOHANNON, dec'd., by Joseph Townsend, Admr. 22 June 1816. Among buyers: Polly Bohannon, Joseph Townsend.

Inventory of estate of Hannah NORRIS, dec'd., widow of John Norris, dec'd., by William Norris.

Page 311

Inventory of estate of John Withers, dec'd., by Ambrose Porter and Enoch K. Withers, Extrs. Four slaves.

Page 312

Sale of estate of MOURNING WINN, dec'd., by Peter Winn, Admr. 14 June 1816. Among buyers: Peter Winn, Richard Winn, Miss Patsy Winn, Miss Jane Winn, Mrs. Winn, Miss Martha Winn.

Page 313

Inventory of estate of Henry BUTLER, dec'd., by Elijah Russell.

Sale of estate of Theophilus REDDETT, dec'd., by James Blakemore, Admr. Among buyers: Rachel Reddett.

Page 314

Sale of estate of Thomas DUREN, dec'd., by George Duren. 7 September 1816. Among buyers: George Duren, Joseph Townsend, Peter Townsend.

Page 315

Sale of estate of William WARNER, dec'd., by John Shephard, Admr. 15 June 1816. Among buyers: John Gourley.

Page 316

Supplemental inventory of Joseph MALLARD, dec'd., by David S. Higgason.

Record of division of negro estate of Joseph MOTHERAL, de'cd. To Mary Motheral - 1 slave; to Joseph Robb - 1 slave; to Will Glover - 1 slave; to Robert Hodge - 2 slaves.

Page 317

Year's allowance for widow and family of James CALDWELL, dec'd.

Inventory of estate of Robert DESHA, Sr., dec'd., by Robert Desha, Jr. and J. Winchester. Forty-one negroes; notes on: Edward Alexander, Desha and Shelby, Robert Desha, Jr.(among others).

Page 318

Sale of estate of Richard G. GILLESPIE, dec'd., by George Gillespie, John Shelby, Admrs. Among buyers: George Gillespie, Polly Gillespie, John Gillespie, John Shelby, Henry Bledsoe.

Page 319

Settlement of estate of Nathaniel PARKER, dec'd. Settlement of 29 July 1814: $1092.98. Second settlement: voucher on Robert Parker. List of legatees: Nathaniel Parker, Robert Parker, John Parker, John C. Beeler, Isaac Parker, Thomas Parker, Richard Parker.

Inventory of estate of John DOWELL, dec'd., by Benjamin F. Dowell, Admr.

Page 320   FEBRUARY TERM 1817

Inventory of estate of Frederick MASSEY, dec'd., by John Sloan. 120 acres, 10 negroes; notes on: Adkins Massey.

Inventory of estate of Samuel BEARD, dec'd., by D. Beard and Mary W. Beard, Admrs. Three negroes.

Page 321

Inventory of estate of Martha ALVIS, dec'd., by Ashley Alvis. 16 acres and 106 poles.

Inventory of estate of Samuel ARMSTRONG's heirs, by John Gillespie, gdn.

Inventory of estate of Jane WATWOOD, dec'd., by Hestor Williams.

Inventory of estate of Richard HALL, dec'd., by W. Hall, Extr. Five negroes; notes on: Richard Hall, Jr.

Page 322

Inventory of estate of Walter CARTER, dec'd. 24 January 1817.

Inventory of estate of William HINSON, dec'd., by John Hinson, Extr. 125 acres.

Page 323

Sale of estate of Henry Butler, dec'd., by Elijah Russell, Admr. 16 December 1816. Among buyers: Polly Butler, John McReynolds.

Settlement of estate of John F. CARR, dec'd., by King Carr, Admr. Voucher on Jack F. Carr.

Page 324

Sale of estate of John WITHERS dec'd., by Ambron Porter and Enoch K. Withers, Extrs. 2 January 1817. Among buyers: Catherine Withers, E. K. Withers, Hugh H. Withers, Thomas Withers, E. Withers.

Supplemental account of sale of estate of Joseph MALLARD, dec'd., by David T. Higgason, Admr. 20 December 1816.

Page 325

Sale of estate of James DOWELL, dec'd., by Benjamin F. Dowell, Admr. 19 December 1816. Among buyers: Mrs. Susan Dowell, Benjamin Dowell, Eleazor Dowell, Reuben Dowell.

Page 326

Year's allowance for the widow and family of Henry BUTLER, dec'd.

Settlement of estate of Robert ANDERSON, dec'd., by John Goudy, Admr.

Inventory of estate of George DUTY's heirs by George Gillespie, Gdn.

Page 327

Settlement of estate of Jonathan ROGERS, dec'd, by Griswold Latimer, Admr. 25 December 1816. "...his pay for services in United States Army - $97.50."

Settlement of estate of Stanton ROGERS, dec'd., by Samuel Rogers and Griswold Latimer, Admrs. 25 December 1816. "...for his services in the Army of the United States - $11.06¼".

Page 328

Sale of estate of Nathaniel S. ANDERSON, dec'd. "...the inventory on file of inventories returned to February Term 1787 it being too lengthy to record at full length."

Sale of estate of William MARTIN, dec'd., by Oliver Martin, Extr. Two sales: 28 June 1816 and 15 January 1817.

Page 329   MAY TERM 1817

Sale of estate of Drury STONE, dec'd., by John Hunley, Admr. Hire of 3 slaves. Among buyers: John Stone, Griffin Bennett, Richard Sneed, "Griffin Bennett rents the house and plantation of 40 acres."

Inventory of estate of Peter LEMONS. dec'd., by John Lemmons, William Lemmons, A. Hicks, Extrs. "...an improvement on Congress land in Giles County of about 13 acres;" note on William Lemmons, John Lemmons.

Page 330

Sale of estate of Frederick MASSEY, dec'd., by John Sloan, Admr. Seven negroes. Among buyers: John Sloan, James G. Sloan, Hezikiah Sloan.

Page 331

Inventory of estate of William MAYS, dec'd., by James McElroy, Admr. "...pay due from the United States for the performance of a tour of duty of six months in the militia of Tennessee in Capt. Neal's Company."

Page 332

Sale of estate of Robert OVERSTREET, dec'd., by Josiah Crain. 1 June 1816. Among buyers: Patsey Overstreet, Josiah Crain.

Page 333

Inventory of estate of heirs of William COCHRAN, dec'd., by John Cochran. Four slaves "hired the year 1813," Three slaves "hired the year 1814."

Sale of estate of Jane WATWOOD, dec'd., by Hector Williams, Admr. "Edward Williams security for his negro Jack for $3.83.

Inventory of estate of Samuel ROBB, dec'd., by Samuel Stewart, Admr. "...wages drawn from the paymaster for his services as a militia man in Capt. Scurry's Co."

Page 334

Sale of estate of Drury STONE, dec'd., by John Hunley. 28 June 1816. Among buyers: John Stone, Joseph Townsend, Peter Townsend, Richard Stone. Three slaves. "Griffin Bennett rents the house and plantation of 40 acres for $80.00."

Page 335

Year's allowance for widow and family of Isaac DAY, dec'd.

Supplemental inventory of estate of Daniel LEGGET, dec'd., by Richard Garrison, Admr. "$68.50 received on a judgement Jeremiah Legget against John Legget appearing to be the property of said David Legget, dec'd."

Settlement of estate of Theophilus Reddett, dec'd., by James Blackemore and Rachel Reddett, Admrs.

Settlement of estate of Daniel Legget, dec'd., by Richard Garrison, Admr. "Cash drew for said Legget's pay in the militia - $44.50." "...a due bill on Whitmal Legget - $23.00, ...$68.50 received on a judgement against John Legget."

Page 336

Settlement of estate of Robert OVERSTREET, dec'd.

Record of division and allotment of negroes between the divisees of William MCKENNE, dec'd. Property divided between the following legatees: Allen Groves, Nathaniel Rice, Thomas Lemmons, and Bennet Uzzel. To Allen Groves: 5 slaves and $27.50 from each of the other legatees; to Nathaniel Rice : 2 slaves; to Thomas Lemmons 2 slaves; to Bennet Uzzel: 3 slaves, and "Bennet Uzzel shall pay Nathaniel Rice $29.66 and Thomas Lemmons $66.66."

Page 337

Settlement of estate of Stephen WINCHESTER, dec'd., by James Winchester and George Roberts, extrs.

Inventory of estate of Samuel BARR, dec'd., by Joseph McElwrath, Sr., and Joseph McElwrath, Jr.

Page 338   AUGUST TERM 1817

Inventory of estate of Dr. Richard G. GILLESPIE, dec'd., by George Gillespie, Admr. November 1816. (many notes due estate); among buyers at sale: John Gillespie, W. G. Gillespie, George Gillespie.

Page 339

Inventory of estate of Thomas BRINKLEY, dec'd., by William Smith.

Sale of estate of Robert B. Moore, dec'd., by Zachariah Green and Margaret Moore, Admrs.

Settlement of estate of Robert GARNER, dec'd., by Jane Garner, Admr. Note on Marian Garner.

Page 340

Sale of estate of Daniel Legget, dec'd., by Richard Garrison. Among buyers: Sally Legat.

Settlement of estate of William PARR, dec'd., who was Admr. of Joseph MCDANIEL, dec'd., by James Walton, Admr. 28 July 1817.

Settlement of estate of William PARR, dec'd., who was Admr. of Collin ADAMS, dec'd., by James Walton, Admr. 28 July 1817.

Page 341

Settlement of estate of Isaac Day, dec'd., 25 July 1817.

Settlement of estate of Ezekiel LINDSEY, dec'd., by Nancy Lindsey, Admr. "She has paid out of the estate to Berry R. Stark who has intermarried with one of the legatees of said estate $89.22."

Settlement of estate of Samuel LUNSFORD, dec'd., by Humphrey Bate, Admr.

Settlement of estate of Jeremiah HAIL, dec'd., by Richard Carr, Admr.

Page 342   NOVEMBER TERM 1817

Year's allowance for the family of Samuel BARR, dec'd.

Inventory of estate of Elisha CLARY, dec'd., by Hubbard Saunders, Admr. Two negroes.

Inventory of estate of Thomas BARR, dec'd., by John Barr and Polly Barr. 75 acres on Bledsoe Creek, one negro.

Page 343

Inventory of estate of William P. YOUREE, dec'd., by F. Youree and Nancy Youree, Extrs.

Inventory of estate of Jepthah RICE, dec'd., by Nancy Rice.

Sale of estate of Absalom CLOAR, dec'd., by John Hubert, Extr. "...last return made to the court of Sumner County 1813...,"..."sold to Fleming G. Thurman 100 acres," "sold to Terisha Stovall 14 acres." Two negroes hired out 1814-1817.

Page 344

Sale of estate of Samuel BARR, dec'd., by Joseph McElwrath. 18 September 1817. Among buyers: Sarah Barr, James Barr.

Settlement of estate of D. PHILLIPS, dec'd., by Patsey Phillips, Admr. 30 May 1817.

Page 345

Sale of estate of William PURVIS, by Cullen Purvis. 27 December 1816. Among buyers: Allen Purvis, Cullen Purvis, Miles Purvis.

Sale of estate of Thomas BRINKLEY, dec'd., by William Smith. 29 September 1817. Among buyers: Margaret Menter.

Page 346

Settlement of estate of William HENDERSON, dec'd., by John Henderson and John Henson, Admrs. Cash paid to Thomas Henderson, William Henson, Josiah Henson, Solomon Henson.

Page 346

Division and allotment of negroes belonging to the estate of Alexander TENNEN, dec'd., between the heirs of Tennen, 2 September 1817. " to the widow Mary Tennin: one negro man; to Jane Hassle, 1 negro girl; to Betsey Cavitts, 1 negro girl, to Sevran Tennin, 2 negro children, to James Tennin, 1 negro man, to Polly Tennen, 1 negro girl."

Page 347

Settlement with guardian of heirs of William COCHRAN, dec'd., John Cochran, Gdn. 20 May 1817.

Settlement of estate of West Edwards, dec'd., by Thomas F. Edwards, Admr.

Supplemental inventory of estate of David WATSON, dec'd., by John Hall, Admr. Blacksmith tools.

Supplemental inventory of estate of Joseph BARRON, dec'd., by Dabney Finley, Extr.

Page 348   FEBRUARY TERM 1818

Inventory of estate of Col. William TRIGG, dec'd., by Will Trigg, Jr., Extr. 18 November 1817. Nineteen negroes. Notes on Will Trigg, Edward Sanders, S. K. Blythe, Polly Quarles, Hadin Trigg, Alonson Trigg, Daniel Trigg. Property left the use of Mrs. Sarah Trigg 1 December 1817: 11 slaves.

Page 349

Inventory of estate of Abner BALL, dec'd., by Isaac Ball. Notes owed to..."Bank on Ellixander, Nashville Bank, Baltimore, Knoxville, Kentucky, Frankfort, Richmond, Virginia, Cape Fear, Wilmington, State Bank North Carolina.

Sale of estate of Thomas BARR, dec'd. 75 acres, 1 negro. Among buyers: widow Polly Barr, John Barr.

Page 350

Sale of estate of Jeptha RICE, dec'd., by Nancy Rice.

Page 351-352

Sale of estate of John NORRIS, dec'd. 31 March 1815. Among buyers: Nancy Norris, Stephen Norris, Thomas Norris, Samuel Norris, George Norris, James Norris, William Norris, Hannah Norris. Second sale 13 December 1816: among buyers: Elizabeth Jones.

Page 353

Sale of estate of Thomas NORRIS, dec'd., by William Norris. 28 March 1816. Among buyers: William Norris, Samuel Norris, James Norris, Stephen Norris, George Norris.

Sale of estate of Hannah NORRIS, 15 December 1816, by William Norris, Admr. Among buyers: William Norris, Elizabeth Jones, Stephen Norris, George Norris.

Page 354

Sale of estate of Rowland HOOD, dec'd, by Mary Hood, Admr. 23 March 1816. Among buyers: Maryann Hood, Mary Hood.

Page 355

Sale of estate of Elisha CLARY, dec'd., by Hubbard Saunders, Admr. Among buyers: Mrs. Clary.

Page 356

Inventory of estate of Starky DAUGHTERY, dec'd., by Robert Lawrence. 31 January 1818.

Current account between orphans of Stephen PITT, dec'd. and Davis Pitt, Guardian. Hawkins Pitt and Eliza Pitt, orphans of Stephen Pitt; accounts beginning 1 June 1816.

Inventory of estate of Mathew HART, dec'd., by William Hart.

Page 357

Inventory of estate of Theophilus HUNTER, dec'd., by John Parnel, Edith Hunter, Admrs.

Settlement of estate of Joseph BARRON, dec'd. Dabney Finley, one of the Extrs. Accounts and notes: Mrs. Harrison, Mrs. Elender M. Night, Mrs. Jackson, Mrs. King.

Page 358

Year's allowance for widow and children of Elisha Clary.

Settlement of estate of Absalom CLOAR, dec'd., by John Hubbert, Extr.

Page 359

Division of negroes belonging to the estate of Theophilus REDDETT, dec'd. between his heirs: to M. D. Reddett, 1 negor; to William Reddett, one negro; to Sally Reddett, 1 negro; to Stark 2 negroes; to Theophilus Reddett, 1 negro; to William Lytle, 1 negro.

Record of current account of William H. Anderson, Gdn. for William GLASGOW.

Record of current account of John Gillespie, Gdn for heirs of Samuel ARMSTRONG, dec'd.

Year's allowance for widow and family of Jeptha RICE, dec'd.

Page 360

Division and allotment of negroes between the heirs of William Dodson, dec'd.; to Katherine D. Dodson, 2 negroes; to Nancy Ellis, 1 negro; to Jeney Turner, 2 negroes; to Elizabeth Dodson, 1 negro; to Polly Dodson, 1 negro; to William Dodson, 2 negroes; to Sophronia Dodson, 1 negro; to Edward Dodson, 2 negroes.

Settlement of estate of James NORVELL, dec'd., by Jesse Sheen, Admr.

Page 361   MAY TERM 1818

Settlement of estate of Richard G. GILLESPIE, dec'd. George Gillespie, Admr. Vouchers on: Sally Sanford, Jacob Gillespie, Emelia Swan, "Richard Gillespie to Duty heirs."

Sale of estate of James CLARK, dec'd., by Mary Clark, Joseph Hodge, William C. Anderson, Extrs. 6 October 1809. Four negroes.

Page 362

Inventory of estate of Daniel KELLY, dec'd., by M. Neale, Admr.

Page 363

Inventory of estate of Meredith Crenshaw, dec'd., by Elizabeth Crenshaw, Admr.

Page 364

Sale of estate of Theophilus HUNTER, dec'd., by John Parnal and Edy Hunter, Admrs. 17 March 1818. Among buyers: Eda Hunter, Needham Hunter.

Page 365

Sale of estate of Starky Dottery, dec'd, by Robert Lawrence, Admr. 10 March 1818. Among buyers: Lydia Dottery, Nancy McDaniel, Charity Tilley.

Inventory of estate of Lydia DOTTERY, dec'd., by Stephen Forrester, Extr.

Sale of estate of Matthew HART, dec'd., by William Hart, Admr.

Page 366

Sale of estate of Abner BALL, dec'd. Among buyers: Polly Ball, widow; Isaac Ball; James Ball.

Page 366-367

Sale of estate of Robert HARRIS, dec'd., by Greenberry Orr, Extr. 28 March 1817. Among buyers: Thomas L. Harris, Martha S. Harris, Blair Harris, Mary G. Harris, Elizabeth H. Harris.

Page 368

Inventory of estate of Abigail CLARK, dec'd., by John Sloan and James G. Sloan. 30 acres, 1 negro.

Inventory of estate of Richard SNEAD, dec'd., by Jane Snead and Woodson Winn, Admrs. One negro. Note on Mumford Snead and Elijah Day.

Page 369

Supplemental inventory of estate of Theophilus REDDET, dec'd. by James Blakemore, Admr. "hire of the negroes of the estate of Theophilus Reddet, dec'd for the years 1814, 1815, 1816, 1817....8 slaves. Among hirers: Rachel Reddet, David Reddet.

Division and allotment of negro estate of Charles Elliot, dec'd, by David Shelly. " to Joseph T. Elliston in right of his wife Elizabeth late the widow of said dec'd. - 4 negroes; to Elijah Boddie in right of his wife Maria Boddie, the daughter of said dec'd. - 7 negroes.

Settlement of estate of David HENRY, dec'd. Moses Henry, Samuel Henry, Admrs. Vouchers on Moses Henry, Samuel Henry, Margaret H. Henry, William Henry. "hire of a negro man one year."

Page 370

Settlement of estate of George DUTY, dec'd. George Gillespie, Admr. Vouchers on Eliza Duty. Hire of several negroes. "note of the widow." 1817-rent of heirs' land.

Settlement of estate of John Dowell, dec'd., by Benjamin Dowell, Admr.'

Settlement of estate of Ezekiel LINDSEY, dec'd.

Page 371

Settlement of estate of William WARNER, dec'd., by John Shephard, Extr.

Settlement of estate of Porter ALLEN, dec'd., William Trigg, Jr., Admr.

Settlement of estate of Adam CRUMP, dec'd. William Trigg, Jr., Admr.

Page 372

Inventory of estate of heirs of George DUTY, dec'd., by George Gillespie, Gdn. Four negroes hired 1818.

Settlement of estate of Hugh GOURLEY, dec'd.

Settlement of estate of Samuel WILSON, dec'd., Jonathan Wilson, Israel Moore, Extrs.

Page 373   AUGUST TERM 1818

Settlement of estate of Henry BRADFORD, dec'd., by Henry C. Bradford, Admr.

Settlement of estate of Marian GARDNER, dec'd., by John Sloan, John Barr, Extrs.

Sale of estate of Lydia DOTTERY, dec'd., by Stephen Forrester, Admr. 13 June 1818.

Page 374

Inventory of estate of John WHITLOCK, dec'd., by Nancy Whitlock and John Durham, Admrs. Three negroes.

Settlement of estate of Joseph MALLARD, dec'd., by David Higgison, Admr.

Page 375

Settlement of estate of Moses YOUNG, dec'd., by Josiah E. Giles, Admr. Note on Moses Young, Samuel Young.

Settlement of estate of James CLARK, dec'd., by Mary Clark and William Anderson, EXtrs.

Supplemental inventory of estate of Thomas BRINKLEY, dec'd., by William Smith, Admr.

Settlement of estate of William GEORGE, dec'd., by Jesse Hunt, Admr. "...1814 by cash paid Jesse George on note.."

Page 376

Inventory of estate of Owen DILLARD, dec'd., by John B. Dillard and Gabriel Dillard, Extrs. 50 acres and 80 acres.

Page 377

Sale of estate of Abigail CLARK, dec'd., by James G. Sloan. 30 acres. "John Sloan 1 boy hired."

Page 378

Sale of estate of Richard SNEAD, dec'd., by Woodson Winn and Jane Snead, Admrs. 22 June 1818. Among buyers: Mrs. Jane Snead, William Snead.

Inventory of estate of Thomas BLOODWORTH, dec'd., by Sally Bloodworth. Account on Thomas Bloodworth, "...in the hands of William Bloodworth - $8.00..."

Settlement of estate of Joseph GEORGE, dec'd., by David George, Admr.

Page 379   NOVEMBER TERM 1818

Inventory of estate of Cornelius HERNDON, dec'd., by W. Herndon and J. Winchester. 12 October 1818. Nine negroes.

Inventory of estate of Jonathan WHITE, dec'd., by Polly White. one negro. "1 account Mrs. Polly Thomas."

Page 380

Inventory of estate of Henry MITCHEL, dec'd., by John Mitchel and Archabald Mitchel.

Supplemental inventory of estate of Thomas BRINKLEY, dec'd.

Page 381

Inventory of estate of George GILLESPIE, dec'd., by John Gillespie and Jacob Gillespie. One negro.

Sale of estate of Owen DILLARD, dec'd., 11 September 1818, by John B. Dillard and Gabriel Dillard, extrs. Four negroes. Among buyers: John B. Dillard.

Page 382

Inventory of estate of Griffeth DICKENSON, dec'd., by Wiley Dickenson, and Matilda Dickenson, admrs.

Page 383

Inventory of estate of Robert CARROLL, dec'd., by Sally Carroll and Thomas Carroll, Admrs. "...a number of slaves."

Inventory of estate of William YOUREE, dec'd., by Nancy Youree. Four negroes. Notes on:....Mary Youree, Nancy Youree, Frances Youree.

Inventory of estate of Champion STEPHENS, dec'd., by Elizabeth Stephens.

Supplemental inventory of estate of Robert DESHA, by James Winchester and Robert Desha, Extrs.

Page 384

Inventory of estate of James WILSON, dec'd., by Thomas Wilson.

Inventory of estate of Robert ELLAW, dec'd., by Dianah Ellaw. Three negroes.

Page 385

Inventory of estate of John CALDWELL, dec'd., by James Roney, Admr.

Supplemental inventory of estate of John WHITLOCK, dec'd, by John Durham and Nancy Whitlock, ADMRS. "...owing in the State of Kentucky..."

Sale of estate of John WHITLOCK, dec'd., by John Durham and Nancy Whitlock, Admrs., 9 September 1818.

Settlement of estate of Enos KING, dec'd., ..."a man of color"..., by William H. Anderson, Admr. 24 September 1818.

Page 386

Settlement of estate of Robert DESHA, dec'd.

Settlement of estate of Mourning WINN, dec'd.

Year's allowance for widow and family of John WHITLOCK, dec'd.

Page 387

Settlement of estate of John NORRIS, dec'd., by Thomas Blackmore and William Norris, Extrs.

Settlement of estate of David WATSON, dec'd. John Hall, Admr. One negro woman.

Page 388

Settlement of estate of Terisha STOVALL, dec'd. William Stovall, Admr. One negro boy. Vouchers on: William Stovall, James Stovall, Sindy R. Stovall.

Settlement of estate of Henry BUTLER, dec'd., by Elijah Russell, Admr. 16 April 1818. Vouchers on:...Henry Butler, Polly Butler.

Page 389

Inventory of estate of Peter SUMMERS, dec'd., by Isaac Armfield, Admr.

Inventory of estate of William R. McDANIEL, dec'd., by William McDaniel, Admr.

Settlement of estate of James CRYER, dec'd. Hardy M. Cryer and John Cotton, Admrs.

Page 390

Sale of estate of Thomas BLOODWORTH, dec'd., 1 October 1818. by Charles White. Among buyers: Edwin Bloodworth, John Bloodworth, Lemuel Bloodworth, Joseph Bloodworth, Sally Bloodworth.

Inventory of estate of William MCCARTY, dec'd., by Mary McCarty, Admr. Eight negroes.

Supplemental inventory of estate of Frederick MASSEY, dec'd. 1 January 1818. "Blair Harris, rent of land"...Nine negroes hired out by John Sloan."

Page 391-392

Sale of estate of Meredith G. CRENSHAW, dec'd. Among buyers: Elizabeth Crenshaw, E. Crenshaw, Jane Farr.

Inventory of estate of Charles LEWIS, dec'd., by A. Lewis, Admrx. and F. K. Blythe, Admr. (includes:) names and dates of birth of 42 slaves.

Page 393   FEBRUARY TERM 1819

Inventory of estate of Jesse PAYNE, dec'd., by Malinda S. Payne and John Booker, Admrs. Six negroes. "Mrs. Sanford and G. Sanford bond $300.00"

Inventory of estate of Thomas PRESTON, dec'd., by Lydia Preston, Extr. Six negroes.

Inventory of estate of John CARPENTER, dec'd., by Jonathan Spooner, Admr.

Page 394-395

Sale of estate of Henry MITCHELL, dec'd., by John Mitchell and Archibald Mitchell. Among buyers: Archibald Mitchell, John Mitchell, Elizabeth Boykin.

Page 396

Sale of estate of Robert CARROLL, dec'd., 19 December 1818. by Thomas Carroll. Among buyers: Sally Carroll.

Sale of estate of Peter WINN, dec'd., by James Elliott. Among buyers: Elizabeth Winn.

Page 397

Inventory of estate of Peter WINN, dec'd., by James Elliott. "not sold: five negores."

Sale of estate of Cornelius HERNDON, dec'd., by J. Winchester and William Herndon. Among buyers: Mrs. Mary Herndon, William Herndon, James Herndon.

Page 398

Inventory of estate of Thomas CURRY, dec'd., by William Curry, John Wallace, Catharine Curry.

Inventory of estate of William BRYANT, dec'd., by John Bradley, Sr., and William Hall.

Inventory of estate of King CARR, Jr., dec'd., by Richard Carr.

Sale of estate of Jeptha RICE, dec'd., by Nancy Rice.

Page 399

Sale of estate of James WILSON, dec'd., 12 December 1818, by Thomas Wilson, Admr.

Inventory of estate of John GWIN, dec'd., by William Gwin, Sr. and James Gwin, Jr., Admrs.

Sale of estate of Jonathan WHITE, dec'd., by MaryWhite and Nathan White, Extrs.

Year's allowance for widow and family of Robert CARROLL, dec'd.

Page 400

Settlement of estate of Robert HARRIS, dec'd.

Settlement of estate of Hugh ROGAN, dec'd. William Hall, Admr. "...paid Nancy Rogan $45.00."

Page 401

Inventory of estate of George ESPRY, dec'd., by Henry Head, Extr. One negro; notes on Robert Espry.

Inventory of estate of Mary BRIGANCE, dec'd., by Charles Brigance.

Supplemental inventory of estate of George GILLESPIE, dec'd., by John GILLESPIE and Jacob GILLESPIE.

Sale of estate of George GILLESPIE, dec'd., 9 December 1818 by John Gillespie and Jacob Gillespie. One negro. "One share in the Sumner Cotton Factory."

Page 402

Sale of estate of George ESPRY, dec'd., 12 December 1818, by Henry Head, Extr.

Supplemental Return of sale of estate of Thomas WINN, by John Hunley, Admr. Three negroes.

Inventory of estate of heirs of Samuel ARMSTRONG, dec'd., by John Gillespie, Gdn.

Settlement of estate of Capt. Samuel BUGG, dec'd., by Anselin D. Bugg, Admr. "....legatees...7 in number.."

Settlement of estate of Frederick MASSEY, dec'd., by John Sloan, Admr. Ten negroes; 120 acres.

Page 403

Division and allotment of personal estate of James CRYER, dec'd., between the heirs. To Mary Cryer: 9 negroes; to Hardy M Cryer, $10,003.70.

Page 404

Settlement of estate of Joseph BARRON, dec'd. Dabney Finley, Guardian for Mary P. Barron and Jane Barron, heirs of Joseph Barron, dec'd.

Settlement with the executors of guardian of heirs of George DUTY, dec'd. "cash on hand for negro hire..$14.56; to balance of account allowed to Eliza Duty..$17.75." George Gillespie, Gdn.

Settlement of estate of Thomas BRINKLEY, dec'd. William Smith, Admr.

Page 405

Division of the negro estate of Daniel SMITH, dec'd. 31 December 1818. To Mrs. Sally Smith: 13 negroes; to Mary Sanders, 20 negroes; to George Smith: 19 negroes.

Sale of estate of Richard SANFORD, dec'd., by Sarah Sanford. Among buyers: George Sanford.

Page 406   MAY TERM 1819

Sale of estate of James PIKE, dec'd., 8 April 1819.

Sale of estate of Samuel BEARD, dec'd., 15 March 1819. One negro woman hired. Among buyers: Mary W. Beard, David Beard, Thomas C. Beard, Adam Beard..

Page 407

Sale of estate of John GIVEN, by William Given and James Given, Admrs. 1 April 1819. Among buyers: William Given, Ezekiel Given, Samuel Given, James Given, Betsey McNeale, Betsy Maxwell.

Page 408

Sale of estate of William MCCARTEY, dec'd., by Mary McCartey, Admrx.

Page 409

Sale of estate of George ESPRY, dec'd., 12 December 1818, by Henry Head, Extr.

Sale of estate of Jesse PAYNE, dec'd., 16 January 1818, by Malinda S. Payne and John Booker, Admrs.

Sale of estate of John CARPENTER, dec'd., 25 March 1819, by Jonathan Spooner.

Inventory of the hire of negroes of Frederick MASSEY, dec'd. Ten negroes.

Record of the appraisement of the negro estate of Frederick MASSEY, dec'd., 27 February 1819. Eleven negroes - $5,500.00.

Page 410

Sale of estate of John CALDWELL, dec'd., 7 December 1818, by James Roney, Admr.

Inventory of estate of William MONTGOMERY, dec'd., by William Montgomery, Extr.

Sale of estate of Mary Brigance, dec'd., 20 March 1819, by Charles Brigance.

Page 410

Further settlement of estate of Davis KING, dec'd. "Sally King widow of Davis King is due more money from the estate of Davis King, dec'd,...because there were only two children heirs of said King living at the time said division was made, one having died previous to that time..."

Settlement of estate of Samuel BEARD, dec'd. Vouchers on David Beard.

Page 411

Settlement with guardian of Penelope D. HORN, orphan, by Thomas B. Horn, Gdn., for 1818 and 1819. Guardian bond in North Carolina - $.60, 1818; guardian bond in Sumner County, TN - $.75, 1818;"Expenses of going to North Carolina and bringing three negroes to Tennessee (46days)."

Settlement of estate of William REED, dec'd., by Henry Reed and Thomas Reed, Admrs. Vouchers: Henry Reed.

Supplemental inventory of estate of John GWIN , dec'd., 1 May 1819, by William Gwin and John Gwin , Admrs. "James Lacky debit to John Gwin , Jr., dec'd.; William Gwin , Sr. debit.

Page 412   AUGUST TERM 1819

Inventory of estate of Jonathan SPOONER, dec'd., by James Gwin , admr.

Inventory of estate of James TROUSDALE, dec'd., by William Bryson and B. Trousdale, Extrs. Five negroes.

Page 413

Inventory of estate of Isaac JONES, dec'd., by Alexander Hutchison.

Inventory of estate of James HART, dec'd., by J. W. Hamilton, John Mills, M. C. Hart.

Inventory of estate of Isaac BOYLES, dec'd., 29 May 1819, by Rachel Boyles, Admrx. One negro..."held by James Boyles."

Page 414-415

Sale of estate of Isaac BOYLES, dec'd., by Rachel Boyles. Among buyers: Rachel Boyles, Robert Shy, John Boyles, Jr., James Boyles.

Sale of estate of James HART, dec'd., 6 July 1819, by J. W. Hamilton, John Mills, W. H Hart. Among buyers: Sarah Hart, William H. Hart, Polly Hart, Samuel Hart.

Page 416

Inventory of estate of Eli GILES, dec'd., 14 August 1819, by Ashley Alvis, James H. Giles. 81 acres.

Inventory of estate of Thomas CARROLL, dec'd., by James Carroll.

Inventory of estate of Drury STONE, dec'd., by John Hurley, Admr. Rent of the plantation...for 1818 and 1819; hire of two negroes.

Settlement of estate of Jeptha RICE, dec'd., by Cones Rice.

Page 417

Settlement of estate of Jonathan PEAIRS, dec'd.

Inventory of estate of Frederick GRIFFEN, Sr., dec'd., 21 February 1819,..."in possession of Charles White."

Page 418   NOVEMBER TERM 1819

Inventory of estate of Francis KETRING, dec'd., by Barbary Ketring and Peter Ketring, Extrs. "...sorrel mare or filly in the possession of Barbary Ketring and Christopher Ketring."

Inventory of estate of Betsey LEE, dec'd., by Isaac Peairs.

Inventory of notes of estate of James HART, dec'd., 22 November 1817, by J. W. Hamilton, W. H. Hart, John Mills, Extrs. "..one note given 14 October 1812 due 1 April 1813 for 5 negro girls."...

Page 419

Inventory of accounts due estate of James HART, dec'd., by J. W. Hamilton, W. H. Hart, John Mills, Extrs. Due the estate by: Henry Hart, Steel Hart.

Page 420

Inventory of estate of John JOHNSON, dec'd., by W. J. Johnson, Admr. Eight negroes.

Page 421

Inventory of estate of John Stowers, dec'd., 9 July 1819, by Catherine Stowers.

Inventory of estate of Samuel CHARLTON, dec'd., 14 June 1819, by Fanny Charlton, Admrx. Seven negroes; note on Abraham Charlton.

Page 422

Inventory of estate of Thomas PATTON, dec'd., October 1819, by John Hamilton, Jacob Houdeshall, David Ormond, Extrs. Account on: J. B. Patton.

Sale of estate of Thomas Patton, dec'd., by John Hamilton, Jacob Houdeshall, David Ormond.

Inventory of estate of John KEY, dec'd., by John Key, Extr. Eight negroes in the hands of Alexander Graham; 1 negro in the hands of Henry Belote, "and claimed by him;" 1 negro in the hands of Stephen R. Roberts, and "claimed by him;" 1 negro in the hands of Daniel McConnel,"and claimed by him;" 1 negro in the hands of Dr. Nathaniel Sanders, and "claimed by him;" 1 negro in the hands of Jacob C. Cook, "mortgaged to him;" 1 negro in the hands of Samuel Vaughn,"on hire;" 1 negro in the hands of Thomas Essex "hired to him;" 1 negro "in my possession;" ...."the Fourth Volume of the Laws of the United States in the hands of Strother Key."

Page 423

Sale of estate of John STOWERS, dec'd. Among buyers: Catharine Stowers.

Inventory of estate of William KEEN, dec'd., by William Woodall, Admr.

Page 424

Sale of estate of Jonathan SPOONER, dec'd., 1 October 1819, by James Gwin , Admr. Among buyers: Eliza Spooner.

Sale of estate of Thomas Carroll, dec'd., Among buyers: James Carroll.

Page 425

Sale of estate of Charles Lewis, dec'd., 29 March 1819, by Ann Lewis and S. K. Blythe, Admrs.

Settlement of estate of John HARGROVE, dec'd. "Account of Amey Hargrove..."

Page 426   FEBRUARY TERM 1820

Settlement of estate of Starkey DOTTERY, dec'd. Vouchers against estate: Margret Harper, Peggy McDougle.

Inventory of estate of Thomas B. HORN, dec'd., by King Parker, Admr. Fifteen negroes.

Page 427

Inventory of estate of Peter BYRON, dec'd., by D. Dunn, Hubbard Saunders. Notes and accounts due estate on: Miss Sally Singleton,21 October 1817; Peter Byron, Jr., Negro Jess, Polly Moor.

Page 428

Sale of estate of Jonathan PEAIRS, dec'd., 17 December 1819, by Karen Peairs. Seven negroes,"two of the negroes were ...led off by William and Henry Peairs, they being the highest bidders."

Inventory of estate of Dolly BLOODWORTH, dec'd., 29 December 1819, by William Bloodworth.

Inventory of estate of James KIRKPATRICK, JR., dec'd., by Joseph Kirkpatrick.

Sale of estate of Eli GILES, dec'd., by John Stephenson. Among buyers: Polly Giles, James H. Giles.

Page 429

Sale of estate of William KEEN, dec'd., 26 November 1819, by William Woodall, Admr. "...plantation rented for $32.00."

Inventory of estate of John EDWARDS, dec'd., by William Edwards.

Supplemental inventory of estate of Willis HUNLEY, dec'd. and Drury STONE, dec'd. Hire of the negroes of the estate of Willis Hunley, dec'd. for the years 1819 and 1820. Hire of the negroes of the estate of Drury Stone, dec'd. for the year 1820.

Supplemental inventory of estate of Jesse PAYNE, dec'd., by John Booker and Malinda S. Townsend, formerly M. S. Payne, Admrs. One negro.

Inventory of estate of heirs of Samuel ARMSTRONG, dec'd. John Gillespie, Guardian. "books and tuition for Zeneth Armstrong and Samuel Armstrong.

Page 430

Supplemental inventory of estate of John KEY, SR., dec'd., by John Key, Jr., Extr. Two negroes, "one in the hands of Josephus H. Conn, the other in the hands of Robert White."

Year's allowance for Mrs. Fanny Charlton, widow of Samuel CHARLTON, dec'd. 1 December 1819.

Supplemental inventory of James WILSON, dec'd., by Thomas Wilson.

Settlement of account of Dabney Finley, guardian for Mary P. Barren and Jane Barren, heirs of Joseph BARREN, dec'd. "receipt of Thompson M. Ewing, husband of Mary P. Barron dated 29 December 1819." Rec'd for house rent in Nashville - $488.00. "For the rent of the brick house in Gallatin - $153.75."

Page 431

Settlement of estate of George LOGAN, William Hall, Extr., and settlement of Hester LOGAN, dec'd., William Hall, Admr. Vouchers: Hester Logan, 14 December 1817.

Settlement of estate of Thomas NEEL, dec'd. Vouchers: S.(?) Neele, Brooks Neele, Ann Neele, Henry Neele, Jeane Neele.

Page 432

Settlement of estate of Daniel KELLEY, dec'd., by Mathew Neele, Amos Goyner, Admrs.

Settlement of estate of Thomas BARR, dec'd., by John Barr and Polly Barr, Admrs.

Page 433

Settlement of estate of William PURVIS, dec'd., by Cullen Purvis, Admr.

Inventory of the hire of negroes of estate of Frederick MASSEY, dec'd. Nine negroes.

Division and allotment of negro estate of Frederick MASSEY, dec'd. among the heirs: to Joseph Winn: 2 negroes; to Rachel Row: 1 negro; to George Winn's heirs: 1 negro; to Adkins Massey's heirs: 3 negroes; to John Winn's heirs: 2 negroes; to Benjamin Winn's heirs: 1 negro.

Inventory of estate of Willie Mitchell, dec'd., 15 December 1819, by Silas Polk, Extr.

Page 434

Sale of estate of Samuel CHARLTON, dec'd., by Fanny Charlton. Seven negroes. Among buyers: Fanny Charlton, Abraham Charlton, James Charlton, Jinnings Charlton.

Page 435

Inventory of estate of John JOHNSON, dec'd., by W. J. Johnson and Will T. Wherry.

Inventory of estate of Thomas Settle, dec'd., by Thomas Essex.

Settlement of estate of Jane WATWOOD, dec'd.

Page 436   MAY TERM 1820

Sale of estate of Jesse PAYNE, dec'd., 10 March 1820, by Malinda Townsend, Admrx. and John Booker, Admr.

Inventory of estate of Michael TROUT, dec'd., by John Trout.

Page 437

Inventory of estate of John DONOHO, dec'd., 16 April 1820, by Yancy Turner. Two negroes.

Sale of estate of Thomas B. HORN, dec'd., by King Parker. Ten negroes. Among buyers: Charity Horn, Mary Daugherty.

Page 438

Year's allowance for support of widow and family of Thomas B. HORN, dec'd., 16 March 1820.

Inventory of estate of Dolly BLOODWORTH, dec'd., 16 March 1820., by William Bloodworth.

Sale of estate of Willie MITCHELL, dec'd., by Silas Polk.

Year's allowance for widow and children of Peter BYRON, dec'd. 13 March 1820.

Page 439

Supplemental inventory of John D. Hannah, Dec'd.

Settlement of estate with Jesse Haynie, guardian for Elizabeth ADAMS. 1815: "cash paid James Adams for boarding." 1816: "cash paid Martha E. Adams..." 13 March 1820.

Page 440

Division and allotment of negro estate of Cornelius HERNDON, dec'd. among the heirs, 1 March 1820: To Henry Herndon: 1 negro; to Polly Herndon: 1 negro; to Mary Herndon: 1 negro; to Joseph Herndon: 1 negro; to Nathaniel Herndon: 1 negro; to Massa Chappel: 1 negro; to William Herndon: 2 negroes. "widow - Mary Herndon."

Page 441

Settlement of estate of Lydia Dottery, dec'd.

Settlement of estate of Richard HALL, dec'd.

Settlement of estate of John D. HANNAH, dec'd.

Settlement with John Sullivan, guardian of the heirs of Walter SULLIVAN, dec'd. ....to allow guardian money to support "the widow and three children of Walter Sullivan..."

Page 442-443

Sale of estate of Peter BYRON, dec'd., 14 March 1820. Among buyers: Peter Byron, Mrs. Byron. By Hubbard Saunders and D. Dunn, Admrs.

Page 444

Year's allowance for widow and family of Michael TROUT, dec'd. 1 March 1820.

Supplemental inventory of John GWIN , Jr., dec'd., by William Gwin and James Gwin , Admrs. Rec'd by Ezekiel Gwin : $33.90.

Sale of estate of Eli GILES, dec'd., February Term 1820, by John L. Stephenson. Among buyers: Polly Giles, James H. Giles.

Page 445   AUGUST TERM 1820

Inventory of estate of James C. WILSON, dec'd., by Jonathan Wilson, Shadrach Nye, Extrs. Obligations on John Wilson and Sarah Wilson, on John Durham ("note given to Polly Wilson"). One negro.

Inventory of estate of Nathan MORGAN, dec'd., by Ann Morgan.

Page 446

Inventory of estate of Swain STALCUP, dec'd., by Elijah Stalcup.

Inventory of estate of Robert ELLIS, dec'd., by Sornelling Ellis and Abram Ellis. 102 acres, 80 acres, 16 acres.

Page 447

Inventory of estate of William R. MCDANIEL, dec'd., by William McDaniel, Admr. Six negroes. Account on Joseph McDaniel.

Inventory of estate of David HUTCHISON, dec'd., 19 May 1820. One negro.

Page 448

Inventory of estate of Thomas NORVELL, dec'd., by Jesse Sheen, Admr. Three negroes which "were the property of him by bargain and sale or deed of gift from William Martin for and during the lifetime of the mother of the dec'd., Sukey Martin."

Sale of a negro woman and child of estate of Frederick MASSEY, dec'd. "which was allotted to Joyce Massey one of the heirs of said dec'd." John Sloan, Admr and Gdn of Joyce Massey, "who is a minor orphan..."

Return of sale of negro woman and child belonging to estate of Frederick MASSEY, "drawn by Joyce Massey, legatee. Said negroes sold by order of court May Term 1820 and sold 7 June 1820 for $320.00 out of which there is $156.60 due to Admr. for money paid on the other legatees, leaves a balance of $163.30 due said Joyce Massey."

Inventory of estate of William B. PEAIRS, dec'd. and Henry PEAIRS, his partner; 160 acres, 2 negroes.

Inventory of estate of James GOODMAN, dec'd., by Clabourn Goodman, Admr. One negro "now in the possession of John Hazlet."

Inventory of estate of John M. TYREE, dec'd., by William Tyree. One negro.

Year's allowance for widow and family of John CARPENTER, dec'd., appropriated by Jonathan Spooner, Admr.

Page 449

Year's allowance for widow of Jonathan SPOONER, dec'd.

Division and allotment of estate of James CLENDENING, dec'd. per will of dec'd., distributed by David Shelby to the legatees: to Anthony B. Clendening: 5 negroes; to William Patterson: 5 negroes; to James H. Patterson: 5 negroes; to James H. Patterson, Gdn. for Eliza Clendening: 5 negroes. By David Shelby and Henry R. Bledsoe, Extrs.

Page 450

Inventory of notes, obligations, cash of the estate of James CLENDENING, dec'd., by Henry R. Bledsoe and David Shelby, Extrs. Note on Anthony B. Clendening, "son of the dec'd."

Page 451

Settlement of estate of Abner BALL, dec'd., by Isaac Ball, Extr.

Settlement of estate of Abigail CLARK, dec'd, 29 July 1820.

Page 452   NOVEMBER TERM 1820

Inventory of estate of John HAWKINS, dec'd., by James L. Hawkins, John Lauderdale, Baker Walsh.

Supplemental inventory of William TRIGG, dec'd., by Will Trigg, Extr. Accounts: Will Trigg, A. Trigg, Abram Trigg, Hardin Trigg. "Sundry property sold this day, 19 October 1819: (among buyers): Will Trigg, Abram Trigg, Daniel Trigg, Alanson Trigg, Hardin Trigg.

Supplemental inventory of Enos BENTHALL, dec'd., by James Vinson, Admr. Three negroes.

Page 453

Inventory of estate of John PARNEL, dec'd., by Lucy Parnel, Admr.

Inventory of estate of Josephus H. CONN, dec'd., by John Brown, Admr. Six negroes.

Inventory of estate of William DAVIS, dec'd., by Robert Davis. 163 acres; 7 negroes, "one half belonging to James Davis." "note due in the state of Mississippi; note due in Kentucky."

Page 454

Sale of estate of Robert ELLIS, dec'd., 26 September 1820. by Surnellan Ellis. 117 acres, 80 acres. Among buyers: Isaac Ellis, Surnellan Ellis, Mede Ellis, Samuel Ellis, Sarah Ellis, Abram Ellis.

Page 455

Inventory of estate of Moses JONES, dec'd., by Nathaniel Parker. "Seven French Pieces."

Settlement of estate of John GWIN, dec'd., by William Gwin and James Gwin, Admrs.

Page 456

Settlement of estate of William B. ANTHONY, dec'd. "Cash rec'd. for the hire of negroes in the years 1814-1820." "One bond on Mrs. Elizabeth Jones." "Cash paid by Admr. for the maintenance and support of the minor children of William B. Anthony, dec'd. for the years 1814-1820."

Page 457

Settlement of estate of Moore STEPHENSON, dec'd.,"who was Executor of the last will of Abram ROGERS, dec'd., by Thomas Rhodes, Admr. "Money paid to the heirs of Abram Rogers, dec'd.: to Sally Rodgers, Nancy Rodgers, Elizabeth Rodgers, Theany Rodgers, James Jackson, married to one of the heirs, and Allen Cotton, one of the heirs." Notes not collected: one on William Rodgers.

Settlement of estate of Thomas NORRIS, dec'd.

Page 458

Settlement of estate of William TRIGG, dec'd., by Samuel K. Blythe, Will Trigg, Extrs.

Settlement of estate of Dolly BLOODWORTH, dec'd., William Bloodworth, Admr.

Page 459

Inventory of estate of George REID, dec'd., by Spencer Holloway, Admr. Twelve negroes.

Page 460

Division of negro property of Jesse PAYNE, dec'd.: to Malindy Townsend, "late wife of Jesse Pain," 1 negro; to Richard Payne, 2 negroes; to Edwin Payne, 3 negroes. 23 May 1820.

Inventory of estate of Amos GOYNE, dec'd., by John Byrns, Admr. Notes on: ...Rachel Allen.

Page 461   FEBRUARY TERM 1821

Inventory of estate of Joseph WALLACE, dec'd., by James Wallace and David Beard, Extrs. The widow's part: "the half of the tract of land she now lives on, also the house ...and 3 negroes..."

Inventory of estate of John MITCHELL, dec'd.

Page 462

Sale of estate of John HAWKINS, dec'd., by John Lauderdale, James L. Hawkins, Baker Walsh. Among buyers: Mrs. Hawkins, Ben Hawkins, James L. Hawkins.

Page 463

Inventory of estate of Henry HART, dec'd. Three negroes "at Edward Bradley's." Notes on (among others): Samuel Hart, Fanny Gibson, Polly Gillespie.

*Page 172

Sale of estate of William M. KING, dec'd., 22 March 1814, by Richard King and Jennett Hassell, Admrs.

INDEX

GUIDE:

1) Page numbers refer to the original pages.

2) All names in capital letters represent the names of the deceased. Minor children are not thus identified in this index.

3) Many, many other names appear in the actual records. Only those names which are the same surname as that of the deceased or the admr/exec have been extracted, plus any females listed. The researcher should refer to the original records for the other surnames involved in these estate proceedings.

4) Watch for possible translation errors, especially with the letters S and L, and T and F. Check all possible spellings and variations. For example: Dottery-Daughtery; Byrum-Byron; Gwin-Givin.

5) Pages 9 through 12 are missing from the original minutes. Also, there are two sets of pages 72 and 73; any names appearing on the second set are followed by asterisks.

INDEX

Adams, COLIN 194,206,340
Adams, ELIZABETH 439
Adams, James 439
Adams, Knox 207
Adams, Martha E. 439
Adams, Peggy 207
Adams, Samuel 207
Adams, Zenos 207
Adkerson, Richard 147
Alderson, JAMES C. 89,178
Alderson, James 89,163,181
Alderson, Jane 89
Alderson, Josiah 89
Alderson, William 89
Alexander, William L. 138,143-4, 212
Alexander, Edward 317
Allen, ORMAN 20
Allen, PORTER 250,291,371
Allen, Rachel 460
Alley, Samuel 96,106
Alvis, Ashley 321,416
Alvis, MARTHA 321
Anderson, Catherine 110,242-3
Anderson, JOHN 173,187
Anderson, John 95, 110, 187
Anderson, NATHANIEL S. 328
Anderson, Pleasant 187
Anderson, Lemma 187
Anderson, Peggy 110
Anderson, Polly 110,242-3
Anderson ROBERT, 95,110,242-3,326
Anderson, Robert 110,242-3
Anderson, Sarah 187
Anderson, William 51,375
Anderson, William B. 173,187,242-3
Anderson, William C. 361
Anderson, William H. 249,272,281-2,359,385
Anthony, John A. 214-15
Anthony, Mark 214-5
Anthony, Susan 214-5, 229
Anthony, WILLIAM B. 214,229,285-6,456
Armfield, Isaac 389
Armstrong, Elizabeth 20
Armstrong, Magdalene 20
Armstrong, Knox 256
Armstrong, Margaret 256
Armstrong, Samuel 256,429
Armstrong, SAMUEL 146,153,177,207,256,321,359,402,429 **+ 17, 20**
Armstrong, Zenos 265,429
Austin, John 214-5
Avent, HARRIS 241

Badget, JOHN, 279
Badget, Nancy 279
Baker, Isaac 91,138,173,247^2
Ball, Isaac 349,366,451
Ball, ABNER 349,366,451
Ball, James 366
Ball,Polly 366
Barnard, Elisha 192,219,234
Barnes, HENRY 189,197-201
Barnes, Nathan 295-6,310
Barr, James 344
Barr, John 162,257,373,342,432,349
Barr, Samuel 137,150-1,152
Barr, SAMUEL 337,342,344
Barr, Polly 342,349,432
Barr, Sarah 344
Barr, THOMAS 342,349,432
Barrett, David 90
Barrett, Thomas 241,256
Barron, Jane 404,430
Barron,JOSEPH 289,307-8,347,357,404,430
Barron, Mary P. 404,430
Barry, James 305
Bate, Hum (Humphrey) 8,298,341
Beard, Adam 406
Beard, D. 320
Beard, David 406,410,461
Beard, Mary W. 320,406
Beard, SAMUEL 320,406,410
Beard, William 265-8
Beard, Thomas 406
Beeler, John C. 319
Belote,Henry 155,422
Bennett, Griffin 329,334
Benthal, DANIEL 273
Benthal, ENOS 301,452
Benthal, LABAN 158,171
Beshears, Asa, Jeney, and Julia 247
Black, Samuel P. 302-3
Blackemore, James 335
Blackman, Elizabeth 256
Blackman, Rev. LEARNER 244,251
Blackman, Learner 164,174-5
Blackman, Mrs. 251
Blackmore, Thomas 387
Blagg, NIMROD 279
Blagg, Mary 279
Blakemore, G. D. 155
Blakemore, George D. 157,212
Blakemore, James 155, 313,369
Blakemore, Thomas 192
Bledsoe, ABRAM 225,238,239
Bledsoe, Henry 225,318
Bledsoe, Henry R. 238,239,449,450
Bledsoe, Isaac 212,225,238,239
Bledsoe, Milly 225,238,239

Bloodworth, Dolly 227
Bloodworth, DOLLY 428,438,458
Bloodworth, Edwin 390
Bloodworth, HENRY 227
Bloodworth, John 390
Bloodworth, Joseph 390
Bloodworth, Lemuel 390
Bloodworth, Sally 378,390
Bloodworth, Thomas 378
Bloodworth, THOMAS 378,390
Bloodworth, William 378,428,438,458
Blythe, S. K. 348,391-2,425,458
Boddie, Elijah 369
Boddie, Maria 369
Bohannon, Polly 310
Bohannon, WILLIE 270,310
Booker, John 393,409,429,436
Boon, James 304
Boon, WILLIAM 230,304
Boren, JOHN 213
Boren, Sarah 213
Boyce, John 41-44
Boyce, JOHN 279
Boyce, Nancy 41-44, 279
Boyce, Nicholas 41-44
Boyce, NICHOLAS 34,41-44
Boyce, Richard 34,41-44
Boyce, Robert 34
Boyce, William 41-44
Boykin, Elizabeth 394-5
Boykin, Delilah 277
Boykin, James 217
Boykin, JOEL 217
Boykin, Mildred 220
Boykin, ROBERT 277
Boykin, SAMUEL 220
Boyle, John 163,181
Boyle, WILLIAM 114
Boyles, ISAAC 413
Boyles, James 413
Boyles, John Jr. 414-15
Boyles, Rachel 413
Bracken, James 14, 55-6,83,87
Bracken, William 55-6
Bracken, WILLIAM 14, 55-6,83,87
Bradford, H. C. 226
Bradford Henry C. 373
Bradford, HENRY 226,373
Bradford, LARKIN 173,247
Bradford, William 173
Bradley, Edward 463
Bradley, John Sr. 398
Bradley, Joshua 8,252
Brandon, Abel 17,20,146,177
Briggance, Catherine 140
Briggance, Charles N. 194,401,410
Briggance, DAVID 184,194,197-201

Briggance, Elizabeth 140
Briggance, ELIZABETH 273,309
Briggance, George S. 140
Briggance, James 140
Briggance, James, Jr. 194
Briggance, John 140
Briggance, JOHN 273
Briggance, MARY 401,410
Briggance, Patsey 273
Briggance, Polly 194
Briggance, William 140
Briggance, WILLIAM 140
Brinkley, THOMAS 339,345,375,380,404
Brown, Jackson N. 66
Brown, James 245
Brown, Joel 75-76
Brown, JOEL 245
Brown, John 453
Brown, Mary 123
Brown, MATHEW 66
Brown, Nancy 24,29
Brown, Polly 29
Brown, WILLIAM 24,29,123,301
Bruce, BARTEMUS 220
Bruce, Robert 214-15
Bryant, WILLIAM 398
Bryson, William 412
Buckham, Andrew 72
Bugg, Anselin D. 263,402
Bugg, SAMUEL 263,402
Burford, M. 134
Busby, JAMES 290
Busby, William 290
Butler, Henry 388
Butler, HENRY 313,323,326,388
Butler, Polly 323,388
Byrn, J. W. 241
Byrn, Lethy 73
Byron, Peter 442-443
Byron, PETER 427,438,442-443
Byron, Peter, Jr. 427
Byrns, John 460
Byrum, MILAND 124
Byrum, MILDRED 107,135

Cage, Loftin 8
Cage, Reuben 92
Cage, Col. William 92
Cage, WILLIAM 92
Caldwell, Hardy 226,242-243
Caldwell, JAMES 242,317,226
Caldwell, JOHN 385,410
Carpenter, JOHN 393,409,448
Carr, Jack F. 323
Carr, JOHN F. 204,323
Carr, King 7,204,323
Carr, KING, JR. 398
Carr, Richard 221,341,398
Carroll, Elizabeth 23
Carroll, James 35,416,424

Carroll, ROBERT 383,396,399
Carroll, THOMAS 416,424
Carroll, Sally 383,396
Carroll, Thomas 383,396
Carroll, WILLIE 23,35
Cartwright, Patience 73
Caruthers, Ezekiel 139,174-175
Caruthers, JAMES 127,131,288
Caruthers, Hugh 129,131,139,165,174-175,221,288
Caruthers, JANE 165,174-175,221
Caruthers, Jane 129,131,288
Caruthers, Margret 139
Caruthers, Sally 139
Caruthers, ROBERT 139
Caruthers, Thomas 139,174-175
Caruthers, William 139
Carter, WALTER 322
Cates, E. 246
Cathey, Elizabeth 73*
Cathey, WILLIAM 73*
Cathy, James 73*
Cavitt, Betsy 346
Cavitt, John 40
Cavitt, Richard 40
Chapman, Benjamin 236
Chapman, E. E. 274-275
Chapman, JAMES 236
Chapman, John 236
Chapman, Philip 236
Chapman, Samuel 236
Chappell, Massa 440
Charlton, Abraham 421,434
Charlton, Fanny 421,430,434
Charlton, Jinnings 434
Charlton, SAMUEL 421,430,434
Clark, ABIGAIL 377,451,368
Clark, ANDREW 263
Clark, JAMES 51,361,375
Clark, Mary 51,375,361
Clary, ELISHA 342,355,358
Clendening, Anthony B. 449,450
Clendening, JAMES 449,450
Clendining, Eliza 449
Cloar, ABSALOM 150-151,156,343,358
Cloar, Elijah 156
Cloar, John 150-151,156
Cloar, John, Sr. 156
Cloar, William 156
Cochran, Ann 39
Cochran, David 38
Cochran, Hiram 39
Cochran, John 8,38,73,134,333,347
Cochran, Rachel 39
Cochran, Sally 39
Cochran, WILLIAM 8,38,39,73,88,134,333,347
Collier, Robert 107,124,135
Conn, JOSEPHUS H. 430,453
Cook, Jacob C. 422
Cooper, Franky 161

Cooper, John 160,161
Cooper, JOHN 160,161
Cotton, Allen 457
Cotton, John 69,70,189,197-201,389
Covington, Elizabeth 305
Cowden, Elizabeth 136
Cowden, James 111,136
Cowden, Josiah 136,332
Cowden, William 136
Cowden, WILLIAM 111,136
Crain, Jonah 272
Crain, WILLIAM 274-275,302-303
Crane, Lewis 117,139,161,274-275,302-303
Craven, William 283-284
Crenshaw, E. 391-392
Crenshaw, Elizabeth 363,391-392
Crenshaw, MEREDITH 363,391-392
Crockett, George 196,208-210
Crockett, Robert 208-210
Crump, ADAM 250,297,371
Cryer, Hardy M. 291,389,403
Cryer, J. 102
Cryer, James 20,72,127,158,305
Cryer, JAMES 265-268,269,291,389,403
Cryer, Mary 403
Culbert, THOMAS C. 196,208-210
Cummings, MOSES 69-70,202
Curry, Catherine 398
Curry, THOMAS 398
Curry, William 398

Daniel, ROGER 57
Daniel, Susannah 57
Daugherty, Mary 437
Davis, Robert 453
Davis, WILLIAM 453
Day, Elijah 368
Day, ISAAC 230,246,335,341
Day, Mumford 368
Day, Philip 228,230,246[2]
Desha, Robert, Jr. 317,383
Desha, ROBERT, SR. 317,383[2],386
Dickenson, GRIFFITH 382
Dickenson, Wiley 382
Dickenson, Matilda 382
Dillard, Gabriel 376,381
Dillard, John B. 376,381
Dillard, OWEN 376,381
Dinning, John 107,109,171
Dinning, Rachel 94,107
Dobbins, John 230,237-238,285-286
Dodson, Mrs. Caty 121-122
Dodson, Edward 360
Dodson, Elizabeth 360
Dodson, Katherine D. 360
Dodson, Polly 360

Dodson, Sophronia 360
Dodson, William 360
Dodson, WILLIAM 115,121-122, 360
Donoho, Charles 73*
Donoho, John 230,237-238,285-286
Donoho, JOHN 437
Dorris, Samuel 19
Dorris, William 24,29,123
Dottery, Lydia 365
Dottery, LYDIA 365,441,373
Dottery, STARKEY 356,365,426
Douglass, Alfred 183,197-201
Douglass, Edward 13,35,152,197-201
Douglass, James 21
Douglass, JAMES 139
Douglass, Jesse 197-201
Douglass, John H. 197-201
Douglass, Peggy 197-201
Douglass, W. 139
Douglass, William 71,197-201
Douglass, WILLIAM 183,197-201
Douglass, William H. 139
Dowell, Benjamin 370
Dowell, Benjamin F. 319,325
Dowell, Eleazor 325
Dowell, JAMES 325
Dowell, JOHN 319,370
Dowell, Reuben 325
Dowell, Mrs. Susan 325
Dunn, D. 427,442-443
Duren, THOMAS 294,314
Duren, George 294,314
Durham, John 374,385,445
Duty, Eliza 33,147,179,370,404
Duty, ELIZA 47
Duty, George 33,46,47,60,147,179,211,256,326,370,372,404
Duty, Jabus 174
Duty, Solomon 46,60
Duty, Weddo 60
Duty, William 46,147
Duty "heirs" 361

Edwards, Eliza 294
Edwards, Elizabeth 265-268
Edwards, JOHN 429
Edwards, Richard 265-268
Edwards, Thomas F. 228,347
Edwards, WEST 228,347
Edwards, West 228
Edwards, William 429
Edwards, William Jr. 69-70,193
Edwards, WILLIAM 193,265-268,294
Ellaw, Dianah 384
Ellaw, ROBERT 384
Elliott, CHARLES 78,80,82,164,171,174-175,256,369
Elliott, Eliza 78,80
Elliott, Elizabeth 369
Elliott, George 82,244,251

Elliott, HUGH 50
Elliott, James 79,80,82,396
Elliott, Mariah 164,256
Elliott, MARIAH 174-175, 256
Ellis, Abram 446,454
Ellis, Isaac 454
Ellis, Mede 454
Ellis, Nancy 360
Ellis, ROBERT 446,454
Ellis, Samuel 454
Ellis, Sarah 454
Ellis, Sornelling 446,454
Elliston, Elizabeth 369
Elliston, Joseph T. 369
Erwin, James 273
Erwin, RICHARD 273
Espry, GEORGE 401,402,409
Espry, Robert 401
Essex, Thomas 422,435
Ewing, Thompson M. 430

Farr, HARRIS E. 106,120,211
Farr, Jane 391-2
Farr, JOHN 186
Featherstone, Charles 159,163,166,242-3,302-303
Felton, Letitia 205
Felton, Letty 186
Felton, WILLIAM 186,205
Finley, Dabney 347,357,404,430
Findley and McNutt 77
Forrest, Isaac 233
Forrester, Stephen 373,365
Fryett, Julia 39
Fryett, JULIA 88

Gamble, Henry 8
Gambling, James 160,254,288
Gardner, Allen 36,66
Gardner, Betsy 36,112,169,253-254
Gardner, BRYANT 36,66,86,112,148,169,208-210
Gardner, Jane 221,253-254
Gardner, MARION 373
Gardner, Martin 36,86,66,112,148,169,208-210
Gardner, MARY ANN 246,252
Gardner, Polly 253-254
Gardner, ROBERT 221,253-254
Gardner, Robert 23
Gardner, Sally 36,112,169
Gardner, William 36,66,86
Garner, Jane 339
Garner, Marian 339
Garner, ROBERT 339
Garretson, Caty 150-151
Garretson, Ephraim 150-151
Garrison, Richard 213,335,340
George, David 278,299,378
George, Isaac 299
George, Jesse 375
George, JOSEPH 278,299,378

George, Lensey 299
George, WILLIAM 270,299,375
Gibson, Fanny 463
Gibson, Samuel 138
Giles, Eli 84-85
Giles, ELI 416,428,444
Giles, Hannah 84,85,158
Giles, James H. 416,428,444
Giles, Josiah E. 180,375
Giles, Josiah G. 164
Giles, NATHANIEL 84,158
Giles, Polly 428,444
Gillespie, George 33,46,60,147,211,256,318,326,338,
    361,370,372,404
Gillespie, GEORGE 381,4012
Gillespie, Jacob 361,381,40,401
Gillespie, John 207,256,318,321,338,359,381,401,402,429
Gillespie, Polly 318,463
Gillespie, Richard 361
Gillespie, Dr. Richard 270,318,338,361,272
Gillespie, W. G. 338
Gilmore, NATHANIEL 20
Givens, Edward 24
Givens, JOHN 407
Glasgow, WILLIAM 138,143-144, 212,359
Glover, William 258,295-296,316
Goodman, Clabourn 448
Goodman, JAMES 448
Goostree, Absalom 192
Goostree, Watson 68
Goostree, WATSON and ELIZABETH 48,68,72*
Goudy, J. C. 187
Goudy, John 326
Gourley, Adam 289
Gourley, HUGH 289,372
Gourley, James 289
Gourley, John 289,315
Gourley, Margaret 289
Gourley, Mary 289
Gourley, Robert 289
Gowdy, John C. 95,110,173,242-243
Goyne, AMOS 460
Goyner, Amos 432
Graham, Alexander 423
Graham, NANCY 160
Graham, Nelly 160
Grainger, MARY ANN 192,219,234
Grainger, William 40,52,94,96
Green, D. 75-76
Green, Daniel 57
Green, David 57
Green, Elisha 233
Green, Michael 221
Green, Needham 227
Green, Zachariah 279,339
Greer, ANNE 79
Greer, James 79

Griffin, FREDERICK 417
Groves, Allen 195,336
Groves, Thomas 195
Groves, THOMAS 195
Gwin, Ezekiel 407,444
Gwin, James Jr. 399
Gwin, John 165,172,235,411,412
Gwin, JOHN 399,411,444,455
Gwin, Samuel 407
Gwin, James 407,424,455
Gwin, William 47,399,407,411,455

Hadley, Joshua 139
Hail, JEREMIAH 341,221
Hail, JOHN 90,93
Hall, Catherine 87
Hall, David 13
Hall, Elizabeth 220,231
Hall, John 280,300,347,387
Hall, RICHARD 321,441
Hall, Richard, Jr. 321
Hall, Robert 26,27,220
Hall, W. 168,182,203,249,255,321
Hall, William 176,218-219,283-284,398,400,431
Hall, WILLIAM 220,231,235
Hamilton, J. W. 413,414-415,418,419
Hamilton, John 422²
Hamilton, WILLIAM 197-201
Hanna, John D. 182,439,441
Hanna, Martha 182
Hanna, William 182
Harder, Jacob 220
Hardy, Henry 230,304
Hargrove, Amey 425
Hargrove, JOHN 251,425
Harper, Andrew 118-119
Harper, Anny 118-119
Harper, Asa 118-119
Harper, James 118-119
Harper, JOHN 118-119
Harper, Margaret 118-119,426
Harris, Blair 74,189²,252,366-367, 390
Harris, E.H. 74
Harris, Elizabeth 189
Harris, Elizabeth H. 366-367
Harris, JOHN 250,298
Harris, M. G. 74
Harris, Martha 74,189
Harris, Martha S. 189,366-367
Harris, Mary G. 189,366=367
Harris, Patsey S. 74
Harris, ROBERT 74,189,190,366=367,400
Harris, Thomas L. 366-367
Harrison, Mrs. 357
Hart, HENRY 463
Hart, Henry 419
Hart, James 73*
Hart, JAMES 413,414-415,418,419

Hart, M. C. 413
Hart, MATHEW 356,365
Hart, Polly 414-15
Hart, Samuel 414-415,463
Hart, Sarah 414-415
Hart, Steel 419
Hart, W.H. 414-415, 418,419
Hart, William 356,365
Hart, William H. 414-415
Harten, James 168
Harten, JAMES 293
Harten, John 293
Hassell, ABRAHAM 15,40,49
Hassell, Benjamin 49
Hassell, Christian 15,16,49
Hassell, Gennet 15,16,40,49,172,280,287
Hassell, James 168
Hassell, John 15-16,49
Hassle, Jane 346
Haw, JAMES 87,150-151,167
Haw, James P. Kelly 150-151
Haw, Nancy 150-151,167
Haw, Samuel 150-151
Haw, Uriel 150-151
Hawkins, Ben 462
Hawkins, James L. 452,462
Hawkins, John 216,256,346
Hawkins, JOHN 451,462
Haynie, Jessie 429
Hazlet, John 448
Head, Henry 401,402,409
Henderson, 233,240
Henderson, Edness 28
Henderson, JOHN C. 28
Henderson, Patsy 240,241
Henderson, Thomas 240,346
Henderson, WILLIAM 233, 240-241,346
Henry, DAVID 264,292,293,305,369
Henry, Margaret H. 369
Henry, Moses 264,292-293,369
Henry, Samuel 264,292,293,369
Henry, William 369
Henson, John 233, 322,346
Henson, Josiah 346
Henson, Solomon 346
Hendson, William 346
Henson, WILLIAM 322
Herndon, CORNELIUS 379,397,440
Herndon, James 397
Herndon, Joseph 440
Herndon, Henry 440
Herndon, Mary 440
Herndon, Mrs. Mary 397
Herndon, Nathaniel 440
Herndon, Polly 440
Herndon, W. 379
Herndon, William 397,440
Hicks, A. 329
Hickison, David 277,374

Higgason, David S. 302-303,316
Higgason, David T. 324
Hobdy, Bethy 73
Hobdy, ROBERT 73
Hodge, Capt. Joseph 18,51,361
Hodge, Robert 316
Hodges, James 101
Hollis, JAMES 173
Hollis, Jesse 173
Holloway, Spencer 459
Hood, Mary 248,354
Hood, Maryan 354
Hood, ROWLAND 248,354
Horn, Charity 437
Horn, PENELOPE D. 411
Horn, Thomas B. 411
Horn, THOMAS B. 426,437,438
Houd, Jacob 1
Houdeshell, Jacob 101,157,422^2
Hough, ANDREW 294
Hough, Vilot 294
House, Balis 75-76,127,305
House, BAYLESS 57,58,66,75-76,304
House, George 75-76 ------House, GEORGE 127
House, James 75-76,304
House, John 3
House, Micajah 3,37
House, Thomas 66,75-76
House, William 75-76
Howard, ALLEN 272
Howard, G. B. 272
Howel, FANNEY 71
Hubbard, John 134
Hubert, John 150-1,156,343,358
Hubert, William 8,38
Humphreys, C.L. 309
Humphreys, ELIJAH 309
Hunley, John 281-2,283-4,306,307-8,329,334,402
Hunley, William 283-4,307-8
Hunley, WILLIS 281-2,283-4,429
Hunt, Jesse 270,299,375
Hunt, Sion 274-5
Hunter, Adam 13
Hunter, Edith 357
Hunter, Edy 364
Hunter, Needham 364
Hunter, THEOPHILUS 357,364
Hurley, J. 259-62
Hurley, John 259-62
Hurley, William 259-62
Hutchinson, Alexander 413
Hutchinson, DAVID 447

Jackson, Mrs. 357
Jackson, James 457
Johnson, James 113,170

Johnson, JOHN 420
Johnson, JOHN B. 274-5,435
Johnson, W. J. 420,435
Jones, DANIEL 188,189,236
Jones, EDMUND 227
Jones, Elizabeth 188,351-2,353
Jones, Elizabeth Mrs. 456
Jones, ISAAC 413
Jones, LEWIS 94,107-8,109,171
Jones, MOSES 455
Jones, Rachel 94
Jones, William 167
Josey, Allen 13,152
Josey, JOHN 13,35^2,152
Josey, Patsey 13
Joyner, Jesse 167

Keefe, Thomas 25
Keen, WILLIAM 423,429
Kelley, DANIEL 362,432
Kelley, JAMES 3,37
Kennedy, A. W. 67
Kennedy, JAMES 246
Kennedy, WILLIAM 67
Ketring, Barbary 418
Ketring, Christopher 418
Ketring, Peter 418
Ketring, FRANCES 418
Kettles, ELIZABETH 231,244
Key, John 422
Key, JOHN 422,430
Key, John Jr. 430
Key, Strother 422
King, Mrs. 357
King, DAVIS 148,153,154,221,410
King, Enos 280
King, ENOS 249,255,272,281-2,385
King, Priscilla 287
King, Richard 148,153,168,172,221,280,287
King, Samuel 168
King, Sally 410
King, William 40
King, William M. 154
King, WILLIAM M. 168,172, 280,287
Kirkpatrick, ABNER 126
Kirkpatrick, Alexander 4
Kirkpatrick, ALEXANDER 4,126
Kirkpatrick, David 4
Kirkpatrick, Fanny 4
Kirkpatrick, Hugh 4,126
Kirkpatrick, James 4, 126,167
Kirkpatrick, JAMES, JR. 428
Kirkpatrick, Joseph 4,428
Kirkpatrick, William 40
Knox, John 17,177

Lack, James 411
Lambeth, William 113
Latimer, Griswold, 229,232,327^2
Latimer, Hugh 131
Latimer, Jonathan 232
Latimer, Lucinda 131
Latimer, ROBERT 131
Lauderdale, JAMES 111,216,256
Lauderdale, John 111,125,153,177,216,218-9,256,452,462
Lauderdale, Jonah 111
Lauderdale, Samuel D. 111
Lawrence, Robert 356,365
Lee, BETSEY 418
Leggett, DANIEL 213,335^2,340
Leggett, David 335
Leggett, Jeremiah 335
Leggett, John 335
Leggett, Sally 340
Leggett, Whitmal 213,335
Lemmons, PETER 329
Lemmons, Thomas 336
Lemmons, William 329
Lewis, A. 391-2
Lewis, Ann 425
Lewis, CHARLES 391-2,425
Lindsey, EZEKIEL 149,341,370
Lindsey, Isaac 117,161
Lindsey, ISAAC 117,139,161,170
Lindsay, Nancy 341
Logan, Mrs. E. 218
Lindsey, ESTHER 249,255,431
Logan, GEORGE 203,218-9,255,431
Loving, HENRY 21
Lunsford, Levy 298
Lunsford, SAMUEL 223,241,298,341
Lunsford, Susanna 223,241,298
Lytle, William 359

Mallard, Elizabeth 277,302-3
Mallard, JAMES 233
Mallard, JOSEPH 277,302-3,305,316,324,374
Malone, Hillery 134
Marcum, JAMES 138,144,287
Marcum, JASPER 224
Markham, Jasper 145
Markham, Joseph 287
Markham, Pleasant 287
Markham, Pleasant M. 145
Markham, Sabrina 145,287
Marlin, Archibald 34,41-44
Martin, Agnes, 81
Martin, James 86,135,211
Martin, Mathew 263
Martin, Oliver 263,328
Martin, Sukey 448
Martin, THOMAS 81
Martin, WILLIAM 263,328
Martin, William 448

Massey, Adkins 320,433
Massey, FREDERICK 320,330,390,402,409,433^2,448^2
Massey, Joyce 448^2
Matt, Joseph 233
Maxey, John 111,136
Maxey, William 21
Maxwell, Betsy 407
May, Cradick H. 231
Mays, WILLIAM 331
McAdams, William 217
McBride, Hugh 222
McCarty, Mary 390,408
McCarty, WILLIAM 390,408
McClelland, Hugh 54
McClelland, Mary 54
McClelland, WILLIAM 54,104,257
McCrilles, ROBERT 241
McConnell, Daniel 422
McConnell, John 154,161
McDaniel, Andrew 227
McDaniel, JOSEPH 227,235,245,340
McDaniel, Joseph 447
McDaniel, Nancy 365
McDaniel, Stephen 227
McDaniel, William 389,447
McDaniel, WILLIAM R. 389,447
McDougle, Peggy 426
McDowell, JAMES 301,306
McElroy, James 331
McElwrath, Joseph Jr. 337,344
McGready, Isreal 285-286
McGready, M. 285-286
McGready, Margaret 285-286
McGrady, WILLIAM 248,285-286
McGrady, John 248,285-286
McKain, James 25,36,75-76,276
McKinne, WILLIAM 336
McKindree, James 223
McMillan, ALEXANDER 226
McMillan, Christine 226
McNeale, Betsy 407
McNutt and Findley 77
McNutt, WILLIAM F. 77
McReynolds, John 323
Melton, DANIEL 96
Melton, William 96
Menter, William 345
Mitchell, Archibald, 380,394-395
Mitchell, HENRY 380,394-395
Mitchell, John 380,394-395
Mitchell, JOHN 221,461
Mitchell, Sol. 221
Mitchell, WILLIE 433,438
Montgomery, William 49,410
Montgomery, WILLIAM 410
Moore, Isreal 205,222,278,372

Moore, Margaret 339
Moore, Polly 427
Moore, ROBERT 279
Moore, ROBERT B. 339
Morgan, Ann 445
Morgan, NATHANIEL 446
Morrison, ELIAS 53,135
Morrison, Jane 53
Motheral, John 79
Motheral, Joseph 79
Motheral, JOSEPH 258,295-296,316
Motheral, Mary 316
Motheral, Sarah 295-296
Murray, Major Thomas 8

Neale, M. 362
Neale, B. 237-238
Neale, Henry 237-238
Neale, James 237-238
Neale, Jane 237-238,285-286
Neele, Ann 431
Neele, Brooks 431
Neele, Henry 431
Neele, Jeane 431
Neele, Mathew 432
Neele, S. 431
Neele, THOMAS 230,237-238,285-286,431
Neelen, THOMAS 278
Neely, Alexander 212
Neely, James 212
Neely, JOHN 212
Neely, William 212
Neil, Mathew 272
Nesbitt, Agness 128
Nesbitt, James 170
Nesbitt, Jeane 113,128
Nesbitt, JOHN 128
Nesbitt, JOHN MADEWELL(MAXWELL?) 113,170
Nettles, JOHN 125,161,177
Night, Elender M. Mrs. 357
Noel, Thomas 212,233
Noel, WILLIAM 212,233
Norman, EZEKIEL 193,204
Norman, Febe 193,204
Norris, George 351-2,353
Norris, Hannah 351-2
Norris, HANNAH 310,353
Norris, James 351-2,353
Norris, JOHN 192,310,351-2,387
Norris, Nancy 351-2
Norris, Samuel 249,351-2,353
Norris, Stephen 351-2,353
Norris, THOMAS 249,353,457
Norris, William 192,249,310,351-2,353,387
Norris, Thomas 351-2
Norvell, EDWARD 305
Norvell, JAMES 269,360

Norvell, THOMAS 448
Norvil, James 305
Norvil, Patsy 305
Nye, Shadrach 445

Ogles, Peggy 172
Ogles, WILLIAM 165,172,235
Oglesby, EDWARD 86,135,211
Ormond, David 422^2
Orr, Greenberry 47,189,257,366-7
Orr, John 257
Orr, JOHN and FRANCIS 163,181,189,255
Orr, Joseph 258
Overstreet, Patsy 332
Overstreet, ROBERT 272,332,336
Owsler, ALEXANDER 264
Owsler, Helen 264
Ozbrooks, Michael 59
Ozbrooks, RUTH 40,59,94,96

Parker, Isaac 146,191
Parker, Isaac P. 116,132,211,319
Parker, John 191,319
Parker, King 426,437
Parker, Judith 130,133
Parker, Nathaniel 132,191,211,319,455
Parker, NATHANIEL 116,132,146,191,211,319
Parker, Richard 132,319
Parker, Robert 132,191,319
Parker, Thomas 116,132,146,191,319
Parker, THOMAS 130,133
Parker, Thomas J. 191
Parnel, JOHN 452
Parnal, John 357,364
Parnel, Lucy 453
Parr, William 112,117,172,194,206,227,245
Parr, WILLIAM 301,340^2
Parson, John 32,45,71,94,162
Patterson, James H. 449
Patterson, William 449
Patton, J. B. 422
Patton, Robert 41-44
Patton, ROBERT 41-44
Patton, Samuel 125
Patton, THOMAS 422^2
Payne, Jesse 460
Payne, JESSE 393,409,429,436,460
Payne, M.S..429
Payne, Malinda S. 393,409
Payne, Richard 460
Peairs, George 293
Peairs, Henry 428,448
Peairs, Isaac 293,418
Peairs, JONATHAN 247,289,293,417,428
Peairs, Karen 293,428
Peairs, Karin Happet 247
Peairs, William 293,428
Peairs, WILLIAM B. 448
Peek, NORMAN 223

Perry, Catherine 5
Perry, George 5
Perry, John 67
Perry, Josiah 5
Perry, R. 224
Perry, THOMAS 5,26
Phar, Ephraim 186
Phillips, DAVID 217,235,344
Phillips, Patsy 217,344
Phipps, Elizabeth 22
Phipps, WILLIAM 19, 22 (Jr.), 72,78,91,138
Pike, JAMES 406
Pitt, Davis 254,356
Pitt, Eliza 356
Pitt, Hawkins 356
Pitt, Henry 160,254,288
Pitt, Joseph 254
Pitt, Nancy 254
Pitt, Robert 254
Pitt, STEPHEN 160,254,288,356
Pitts, Bunton H. 302-3
Pitts, Henry 302-3
Pitts, L. C. 302-3
Pitts, LUNSFORD 159,163,166,242-3,302-3
Poe, Elizabeth 251,278
Poe, WILLIAM 251,278
Polk, John 89
Polk, Silas 247,433,438
Porter, Ambrose 311,324
Preston, Lydia 393
Preston, THOMAS 393
Purvis, Allen 57-58,75-76,345
Purvis, Cullen 310,345,433
Purvis, Miles 345
Purvis, WILLIAM 295-6,310,345,433

Quarles, Polly 348

Rease, Ephraim 25
Redditt, David 369
Reddett, M. D. 359
Reddett, Rachel 313,335,369
Reddett, Sally 359
Reddett(?), Stark 359
Reddett, Theophilus 359
Reddett, THEOPHILUS 155,313,335,359,369
Reddett, William 359
Reed, Hannah 162
Reed, Henry 141-2,277,411
Reed, JAMES 97-8,162
Reed, Thomas 97-8,141-2,162,277,411
Reed, WILLIAM 141-2,277,411,459
Reed, William 162
Reid, GEORGE 459
Rhodes, Thomas 457
Rice, Cones 416
Rice, JEPTHAH 343,350,359,398,416

Rice, Nancy 350,343,398
Rice, Nathaniel 336
Richardson, MARGARET 112,117,172
Rickman, Frances 290
Rickman, NATHANIEL 290
Rickman, Thomas 290
Robb, SAMUEL 333
Robb, Joseph 295-6,316
Roberson, ALLEN 228,246
Roberts, GEORGE 8
Roberts, George 106,120,211,228,237-8,279,337
Roberts, Henry 8
Roberts, John 8
Roberts, Rachel 8
Roberts, Sally 8
Roberts, Stephen R. 422
Robertson, Ann 246
Robertson, Anna 228
Robertson, DAVID G. 193
Robertson, ALLEN 246
Robertson, William 193
Rodgers, Elizabeth 457
Rodgers, Nancy 457
Rodgers, Theany 457
Rodgers, William 457
Rogan, Frances 176
Rogan, HUGH 168,176,400
Rogan, Nancy 176,400
Rogers, Abram 457
Rogers, ABRAM 457
Rogers, Elizabeth 232
Rogers, Hannah 232
Rogers, JONATHAN 213,229,210,327
Rogers, Lucretia 232
Rogers, Ruth 229,232
Rogers, Sally 457
Rogers, Samuel 229,232,327
Rogers, STAUNTON 216,232,327
Roney, James 385,410
Row, Rachel 433
Russell, Elijah 313,323,388
Ruyle, SOLOMON 222

Sanders, DANIEL 52,61,134
Sanders, Edward 102,115,348
Sanders, Hubbard 115,149
Sanders, James 16,134
Sanders, Mary 405
Sanders, Jane 61
Sanders, Dr. Nathaniel 422
Sanders, Peter 134
Sanders, Richard 61
Sanders, Robert 61
Sanders, William Jr. 61,134
Sanford, G. 393
Sanford, George 405
Sanford, RICHARD 185,405
Sanford, Sally 361
Sanford, Sarah 405

Sanford, T. 185
Sarver, George 226
Saunders, Hubbard 342,355,427,442-3
Scurry, Thomas 250,298
Seawell, JOHN 25,102
Seawell, William 153
Settle, THOMAS 435
Shaw, Hugh 13
Sheen, Jesse 48,68,72*,155,269,301,305,306,360,448
Shelby, David 369,449,450
Shelby, John 270,318
Shephard, John 371
Sheppard, John 269,315
Shy, Robert 414-415
Simpson, Charles 30-1,48
Simpson, E. 30-1
Simpson, Elijah 30-1, 162,257
Simpson, Elizabeth 30-31
Simpson, Isaac 30-1
Simpson, JAMES 30-1,48
Simpson, John 30-31
Simpson, Nancy 30-31
Simpson, Robert 30-31,48
Simpson, William 54,104
Singleton, Miss Sally 427
Sloan, Hezekiah 330
Sloan, James G. 330,368,377
Sloan, John 54,104,158,252,320,330,368,373,377,390,402,448
Smith, DANIEL 405
Smith, George 405
Smith, Joshua 223
Smith, Sally Mrs. 405
Smith, William 339,345,375,404
Snead, Jane 368,378
Snead, Richard 329
Snead, RICHARD 368,378
Snead, William 378
Snoddy, David 137,150,151,152
Snoddy, Elizabeth 189
Snoddy, William 150-151
Snoddy WILLIAM 137,150-151,152
Sparkman, THOMAS 173
Spooner, Eliza 424
Spooner, Jonathan 393,409,448
Spooner, JONATHAN 412,424,449
Stalcup, Elijah 446
Stalcup, SWAIN 446
Stark, Berry R. 341
Stark, Jeremiah 149
Stark, JOHN 184
Stark, Sarah 184
Station, Isham 291
Stephens, CHAMPION 383
Stephens, Elizabeth 383
Stephenson, John 428,444
Stephenson, MOORE 457
Stephenson, Moore 15-16,49
Stewart, DANIEL 72
Stewart, James 53,135

Stewart, Samuel 333
Stewart, SAMUEL 278
Stone, DRURY 306,307-8,329,334,416,429
Stone, John 307-8,329,334
Stone, M.(W.) 134
Stone, Richard 307-8,334
Stovall, Bird 281
Stovall, James 281,388
Stovall, Sindy 281
Stovall, Sindy. R. 388
Stovall, TERISHA 224,281,388
Stovall, Terisha 343
Stovall, Thomas 281
Stovall, W. 224
Stovall, William 281,388
Stowers, JOHN 421,423
Stowers, Catherine 421,423
Stranger, Josiah 134
Strator, Jacob 231,244
Strother, James 154,161,184,194,197-201
Strothers, RICHARD 154,161
Stuard, Paton 302-3
Stubblefield, BENJAMIN H 205
Stubblefield, William 205
Sullivan, WALTER 7,441
Sullivent, John 7,441
Summers, PETER 389
Swann, Emelia 361
Swann, Emelia C. 186
Swann, THOMAS 186

Taylor, RICHARD 155,157
Tennen, ALEXANDER 346
Tennin, James 346
Tennin, Mary 346
Tennin, Polly 346
Tennin, Sevran 346
Thomas, Mrs. Polly 379
Thomas, WILLIE 241,256
Thurman, Fleming G. 343
Tilly, Charity 233,246,287,365
Tilly, GEORGE 233,287
Townsend, Joseph 270,307-8,310,314,334
Townsend, Malinda 436,460
Townsend, Malinda S. 429
Townsend,Peter 307-8,314,334
Trail, BASIL 155,240
Trail, Elizabeth 240
Trigg, A. 452
Trigg, Abram 452
Trigg, Alonson 348,452
Trigg, Daniel 348,452
Trigg, Hardin 348,452
Trigg, Mrs. Sarah 348
Trigg, Will Jr. 163,250^2, 291,297,348,371,452,458
Trigg, WILLIAM COL. JR. 348,452,457
Trousdale, JAMES 412
Trousdale,James 50

Trout, John 436
Trout, MICHAEL 436,444
Trumbo, AMBROSE 106
Trumbo, George 106
Turner, Cloar 158
Turner, Jeney 360
Turner, Yancy 437
Tyree, JOHN M. 448
Tyree, William 448

Uzzel, Bennet 336

Vaughn, Samuel 422
Venson, James 301
Vinson, Henry 217,452

Wallace, James 461
Wallace, John 398
Wallace, JOSEPH 461
Walsh, Baker 452,462
Walton, ———— 36
Walton, DRURY 81
Walton, Gracey 81
Walton, Isaac 20,169,173,208-210
Walton, James 301,340^2
Warner, WILLIAM and MARY 269,315,371
Watkins, JAMES 298
Watkins, Robert 298
Watson, Charles 300
Watson, DAVID 280,300,347,387
Watson, James 300
Watwood, Jane 321,333,435
Weathered, James 153,225,238,239
Weir, William 115
Wells, EPHRAIM 18
Wells, Henry 276
Wells, JESSE 25,36,276
Wells, Rebekah 276
Wherry, Will T. 435
White, Archibald 27
White, Charles 390,417
White, Eli 27
White, JAMES JR. 26,27 (Major)
White, John 26,27
White, JONATHAN 379,399
White, Joseph 26
White, Mary 399
White, Narcissa 26
White, Nathan 399
White, Polly 379
White, Robert 27,430
White, William 26
Whitlock, JOHN 374, 385^2,386
Whitlock, Nancy 374,383
Whitworth, SAMUEL 163
Wilks, William 283-4
Williams, BENJAMIN 113
Williams, Edward 333

Williams, Hestor 321
Williams, Hector 333
Williams, Polly 113
Williford, GREEN 96,105,106
Williford, Lucy 105
Willis, Harvey P. 273
Willis, Mary 22
Wilson, Betsy 62-65
Wilson, Cinthey 45
Wilson, David 1,62-5,139
Wilson, Elener 45
Wilson, Ellen J. P. 125
Wilson, Fanny 125
Wilson, Hannah 1
Wilson, James 20,45,263
Wilson, JAMES SR. 1,32,45,71,94,101,125,157,162,430
Wilson, JAMES 384,399
Wilson, JAMES C. 445
Wilson, James C. 62-5,205,222
Wilson, James R. 125
Wilson, Jane 62-65
Wilson, John 52,62-65,222,445
Wilson, Jonathan 1,62-65,165,174-5,205,221,222,372,445
Wilson, Matilda 62-65
Wilson, Moses 45
Wilson, Polly 445
Wilson, SAMUEL 205,222,372
Wilson, Sarah 205,222,445
Wilson, Samuel 1,62-65,222
Wilson, Thomas 384,399
Wilson, William 52,62-65
Wilson, Zacheus 20,157,222
Wilson, ZACHEUS 51,62-65,147,152,158
Wilson, Zacheus, Jr. 62-65,1,125
Wilson, Zacheus, Sr. 1,101
Winchester, J. 228,237-8,287,317,379,397
Winchester, James 39,153,279,337,383
Winchester, STEPHEN 228,237-8,279,337
Winn, Benjamin 433
Winn, Elizabeth 396
Winn, George 433
Winn, John 433
Winn, Joseph 433
Winn, Miss Jane 312
Winn, Miss Martha 312
Winn, Mourning, 259-62
Winn, Miss Patsy 312
Winn, Peter 296,312
Winn, Richard 312
Winn, Woodson 368,378
Wynn, MOURNING 269,312,386
Wynn, PETER 396
Wynn, THOMAS 259-62,402
Withers, Catherine 324
Withers, E. 324
Withers, E.K. 324
Withers, Enoch K. 311,324
Withers, Hugh H. 324

Withers, JOHN 311,324
Withers, John 50
Withers, Thomas 324
Woodall, William 423,429
Wooten, JOHN 283-4
Wyles, JOHN 2,19
Wyles, Sarah 2
Wyles, William 2

Yancey, GARLAND 226,252
Yancy, Polly 252
Yancy, Robert 252
Yancy, Robert H. 226,252
Yancy, Robert 252
Yance, Tyry 252
Yandell, John 302-3
Yandle, Wilson 302-3
Young, Elizabeth 180
Young, HENRY 83
Young, Moses 375
Young, MOSES 164,178,180,375
Young, Nicholas 190
Young, Samuel 375
Youree, F. 343
Youree, Frances 383
Youree, Mary 383
Youree, Nancy 343,383
Youree, Patrick 8
Youree, WILLIAM 383
Youree, WILLIAM P. 343

www.ingramcontent.com/pod-product-compliance
Lightning Source LLC
Chambersburg PA
CBHW080438230426
43662CB00015B/2313